GOODSON MUMBA

The CEO's Diary

On Building a Strength-Based Organization

Copyright © 2024 by Goodson Mumba

All rights reserved. No part of this publication may be reproduced, stored or transmitted in any form or by any means, electronic, mechanical, photocopying, recording, scanning, or otherwise without written permission from the publisher. It is illegal to copy this book, post it to a website, or distribute it by any other means without permission.

First edition

ISBN: 9798334060609

This book was professionally typeset on Reedsy. Find out more at reedsy.com

Dedication

I extend my sincerest gratitude to my beloved wife, Edith Mumba, and our children, Angelina, Lubuto, Letticia, Lulumbi, and Butusho, for their unwavering support and understanding throughout the conception, writing, and eventual publication of this book, despite the sacrifices and challenges they endured.

Contents

Preface		iii
Acknowledgments		v
Dedication		vi
Disclaimer		vii
1	Chapter One: The CEO's Family Time	1
2	Chapter Two: A Glimpse into the CEO's Day's Routine	14
3	Chapter Three: Introduction to Strength-Based Organizations	28
4	Chapter Four: The Foundation of Strength-Based Leadership	46
5	Chapter Five: Identifying and Assessing Strengths	57
6	Chapter Six: Building a Strength-Based Culture	68
7	Chapter seven: Leveraging Strengths for Team Performance	83
8	Chapter Eight: Developing Strengths-Based Talent Management...	97
9	Chapter Nine: Leading Change with a Strength-Based Approach	114
10	Chapter Ten: Measuring and Evaluating Strengths-Based...	130
11	Chapter Eleven: Case Studies: Examples of Strengths-Based...	141

| 12 | Chapter Twelve: Charting the Future Of Strengths-Based... | 146 |
| *About the Author* | | 153 |

Preface

Welcome to "The CEO's Diary: Building a Strength Based Organization." In the pages of this book, you will embark on a journey alongside visionary leaders, exploring the intricacies of organizational excellence and the transformative power of a strength-based approach.

At the heart of every successful organization lies a strong foundation built upon the unique talents and abilities of its people. In today's fast-paced and ever-evolving business landscape, it is essential for leaders to harness the strengths of their teams to drive innovation, foster resilience, and achieve sustainable growth.

"The CEO's Diary" offers a rare glimpse into the inner workings of a modern leader's mind, chronicling the daily challenges, triumphs, and insights of a CEO dedicated to cultivating a culture of strength and empowerment within their organization. Through firsthand accounts, candid reflections, and practical strategies, this book provides invaluable lessons for leaders at every level.

Whether you are a seasoned executive seeking to optimize your organization's performance or a budding entrepreneur navigating the complexities of leadership for the first time, "The CEO's Diary" offers timeless wisdom and actionable guidance to help you unlock the full potential of your team and achieve lasting success.

As you turn the pages of this book, may you be inspired to embrace a strength-based approach to leadership, igniting a spark of innovation and excellence that will propel your organization to new heights. Thank you for joining us on this journey – together, we can build a future filled with limitless possibilities.

Warm regards,

Goodson Mumba

Acknowledgments

I wish to express my eternal gratitude to the Almighty God for the boundless wisdom emanating from His universal consciousness, which enriches our understanding of the world. I also extend my heartfelt appreciation to all those who have contributed to my life's journey, providing spiritual, moral, emotional, and material support.

Dedication

I extend my sincerest gratitude to my beloved wife, Edith Mumba, and our children, Angelina, Lubuto, Letticia, Lulumbi, and Butusho, for their unwavering support and understanding throughout the conception, writing, and eventual publication of this book, despite the sacrifices and challenges they endured.

Disclaimer

This book is a work of fiction. Names, characters, businesses, places, events, and incidents are either the products of the author's imagination or used in a fictitious manner. Any resemblance to actual persons, living or dead, or actual events is purely coincidental.

1

Chapter One: The CEO's Family Time

As the morning light gently filters through the curtains, Howard stirs from his slumber, his mind still heavy with the weight of CEO responsibilities. Blinking away the remnants of sleep, he turns to find Angela, his anchor in the tumult of his life, peacefully sleeping beside him.

With a sudden jolt, realization crashes over him like a tidal wave. Today was not just another day of endless meetings and emails. No, today held a different kind of obligation – a familial duty that he couldn't afford to overlook.

As Howard glances at the clock, his heart quickens its pace. They were expected at Angela's parents' house for a long-overdue visit, a promise they made amidst the chaos of their busy lives. He can almost feel the weight of the promise pressing down on him, mingled with a sense of guilt for neglecting their family time.

Rising from the bed, Howard's mind races as he contemplates the jam-packed day ahead. The emails, the meetings, the deadlines – they all loom over him like menacing shadows. Yet, amidst the chaos, a glimmer of hope emerges – the prospect of a day spent with loved ones, away from the relentless demands of the corporate world.

With a determined resolve, Howard leans over to gently awaken Angela, knowing that together they will navigate through the whirlwind of obligations that await them. Today, amidst the ceaseless hustle of his CEO life, he will carve out a precious moment for family – a reminder of what truly matters in the grand tapestry of life.

With a contented sigh, Angela turns to face Howard, her eyes alight with the dawning realization of the day's plans. "Howard, darling," she begins, her voice a gentle melody that resonates with the quiet anticipation of what lies ahead, "do you think we're ready for today?"

Howard, his gaze softening as it meets hers, reaches out to caress her cheek, his touch a tender reassurance amidst the uncertainty of the day ahead. "I believe we are, my love," he murmurs, his voice a soothing balm that eases the knots of apprehension that threaten to unravel within her. "After all, we've been looking forward to this visit for weeks now."

As they linger in the warmth of their shared embrace, their conversation meanders through the labyrinth of emotions that accompany the prospect of reuniting with loved ones. Memories of past visits dance before their eyes, evoking laughter and tears in equal measure, while hopes for the future intertwine with the tender threads of their shared dreams.

Angela's laughter rings out like a symphony, filling the room with its infectious joy. "Do you remember the last time we visited? Dad's stories had us in stitches for hours!"

Howard chuckles, his heart swelling with love for the woman beside him. "How could I forget? And your mom's cooking always leaves me craving more. I can practically smell her

CHAPTER ONE: THE CEO'S FAMILY TIME

homemade pie already."

Yet beneath the surface of their banter lies an unspoken truth – the recognition of the fleeting nature of time, and the preciousness of moments shared with loved ones. As they prepare to embark on this journey of family, love, and togetherness, Howard and Angela find solace in the knowledge that no matter what challenges may lie ahead, they will face them together, hand in hand, heart to heart.

Their voices, soft and intimate, echo off the walls, carrying with them the anticipation of reunions and cherished moments.

But their tender exchange is interrupted by a sudden rapping on the door, followed by the excited voices of their two youngest daughters, a whirlwind of energy and enthusiasm.

"Mom! Dad!" they cry out, their voices a joyful cacophony that fills the room with the infectious excitement of youth. "Don't forget, we're visiting Grandma and Grandpa today! We've been waiting for this forever!"

Howard and Angela exchange a knowing glance, their hearts swelling with love and pride at the sheer exuberance radiating from their daughters. With a shared smile, they rise from their bed, their steps quickening as they make their way to the door to greet their daughters.

In that moment, amidst the chaos and commotion of family life, Howard and Angela find themselves reminded of the simple joys that await them – the laughter of loved ones, the warmth of familial bonds, and the beauty of shared moments that will be treasured for a lifetime.

Angela swiftly rises from the bed, her footsteps quickening as she moves to answer the door, anticipation mingling with curiosity in her heart.

As the door swings open, their daughters burst into the

room like a whirlwind of energy and excitement, their faces illuminated with pure joy and anticipation. "Mom! Dad!" they exclaim in unison, their voices echoing with the eagerness of youth. "We're going to visit Grandma and Grandpa today, remember?"

With a tender smile, Angela envelops her daughters in a warm embrace, their excitement contagious as it fills the room with an infectious energy. "Of course, my darlings," she reassures them, her voice filled with warmth and affection. "We wouldn't miss it for the world."

Howard joins them, his eyes sparkling with pride as he gathers his family close. "That's right," he adds, his voice resolute and unwavering. "Today, we're making memories that will last a lifetime."

In that moment, amidst the laughter and chatter of their daughters, Howard and Angela find themselves overwhelmed with gratitude for the simple joys of family and the precious moments that bind them together. As they prepare to embark on their journey, they are filled with a sense of anticipation for the adventures that await them and the memories that they will create together, as a family united in love and laughter.

With the first light of dawn painting the sky in hues of pink and gold, Howard stands at the threshold of his home, his heart brimming with anticipation as he watches his family gather before him. Angela, his steadfast companion, stands by his side, her eyes alight with excitement, while their three daughters and son buzz with energy, eager for the adventure that lies ahead.

As they load their belongings into the car, laughter and chatter fill the air, mingling with the soft rustle of leaves and the distant hum of traffic. Howard's heart swells with pride as he looks upon his family, a testament to the love and bond that unites them.

With a final glance at their home, Howard takes Angela's hand in his, their fingers intertwining like the threads of fate weaving them together. "Are we ready?" he asks, his voice filled with a mixture of excitement and anticipation.

Angela smiles, her eyes shining with joy. "More than ready," she replies, her voice carrying the promise of adventure and possibility.

With a sense of purpose and determination, Howard leads his family to the car, each step bringing them closer to the journey that awaits. As they settle into their seats and buckle up for the road ahead, Howard can't help but feel a surge of excitement coursing through his veins.

With a turn of the key, the engine roars to life, filling the air with the familiar hum of anticipation. As they pull out of the driveway and onto the open road, Howard can't help but feel a sense of exhilaration wash over him.

With each passing mile, the landscape unfolds before them like a tapestry, each turn of the road bringing them closer to their destination. As they journey on, laughter and conversation fill the car, weaving together the fabric of their shared memories and experiences.

As they approach Kabwe, the anticipation reaches a fever pitch, each member of the family eagerly awaiting the reunion that awaits them. With a sense of excitement and anticipation, Howard and his family press on, their hearts full of love and anticipation for the moments that lie ahead.

Meanwhile, in Kabwe, Angela's parents stand on the veranda of their home, their eyes fixed on the winding road that disappears into the distance. With each passing moment, their anticipation grows, their hearts fluttering with excitement at the prospect of welcoming their daughter, her husband, and their beloved grandchildren.

As they gaze into the horizon, memories of past visits flood their minds – the laughter echoing through the halls, the warmth of familial bonds, and the joy of being surrounded by loved ones. With each passing car, their hearts skip a beat, hoping that the next one will bring their family home.

Finally, in the distance, they catch a glimpse of headlights, their beams cutting through the darkness like beacons of hope. With bated breath, they watch as the car draws closer, the silhouette of their loved ones becoming clearer with each passing moment.

As the car pulls into the driveway, Angela's parents rush forward to greet their family, their arms outstretched in welcome. Tears of joy fill their eyes as they embrace, their hearts overflowing with love and gratitude for the precious moments they will share together.

In that moment, as Angela, Howard, and their children step out of the car, the air is filled with a sense of warmth and belonging. For in the embrace of family, there is a sense of homecoming – a reminder that no matter where life may take them, their hearts will always be bound together by love.

As the sun begins its slow descent, casting a golden glow over the sprawling yard of Angela's parents' home, the family gathers together under the shade of a towering oak tree. Angela and Howard sit side by side, their hands intertwined, as they engage in lively conversation with Angela's parents.

The air is filled with the soft murmur of voices and the occasional burst of laughter, as the family delves into a wide array of topics. From social issues to investments to politics,

CHAPTER ONE: THE CEO'S FAMILY TIME

no subject is off-limits as they exchange ideas and perspectives with warmth and friendship.

Angela's parents, their faces illuminated by the fading light, listen intently to the insights shared by their daughter and son-in-law, their eyes sparkling with pride at the depth of their knowledge and the passion with which they speak.

Meanwhile, outside in the yard, the children are a whirlwind of energy and excitement, their laughter mingling with the sound of their footsteps as they chase each other through the grass. From tag to hide-and-seek to impromptu games of soccer, they revel in the freedom of the open space, their youthful exuberance filling the air with joy.

As the evening wears on, the conversation continues late into the night, the bonds of family growing stronger with each passing moment. And amidst the laughter and the chatter, amidst the games and the stories, Angela and Howard find themselves grateful for the love and connection that surrounds them – a reminder that in the embrace of family, there is always a place to call home.

As the evening sun casts its warm glow through the windows, illuminating the dining table with a golden hue, Angela, Howard, and Angela's parents gather together for a family dinner. The aroma of home-cooked meals fills the air, mingling with the soft chatter and laughter that dances around the room.

Amidst the clinking of cutlery and the gentle hum of conversation, the topic shifts to Tony, their beloved grandson, who has recently embarked on a new journey as a boarding school student. Angela's father, a figure of wisdom and experience, leans forward, his eyes twinkling with a sense of authority and concern.

"Tony," he begins, his voice carrying the weight of years of experience, "as you embark on this new chapter of your life, remember the values that have been instilled in you from a young age. Stay true to yourself, and always strive to uphold a morally upright lifestyle."

Angela's mother nods in agreement, her eyes filled with pride and affection as she adds her own words of wisdom. "Yes, dear," she says, her voice soft but firm, "remember the importance of honesty, integrity, and kindness in all that you do."

Howard, Angela's husband, joins in, his voice filled with warmth and encouragement. "And don't forget to work hard and stay focused on your studies," he adds, his gaze meeting Tony's with a sense of unwavering support.

Angela, Tony's mother, smiles warmly, her heart overflowing with love and pride for her son. "We believe in you, Tony," she says, her voice brimming with confidence. "You have the strength and the resilience to overcome any challenges that come your way."

As the conversation continues late into the night, the bonds of family grow stronger with each passing moment. And amidst the laughter and the love, amidst the shared memories and the shared dreams, Angela, Howard, and Angela's parents find themselves grateful for the gift of family – a beacon of light and love that guides them through life's journey, every step of the way.

As the clock ticks towards midnight, the soft glow of the lamp casts a gentle radiance over the room, illuminating the faces of the family gathered around the cozy living space. Angela's mother, a figure of warmth and wisdom, rises from her seat with a soft rustle of her skirts.

"Children," she begins, her voice carrying the gentle authority of generations past, "it's time for us to bid the day farewell and embrace the restful embrace of sleep. Tomorrow holds new adventures, and we must be ready to meet them with open hearts."

Her words hang in the air, a gentle reminder of the fleeting nature of time and the preciousness of each moment shared together. Angela, Howard, and their children exchange knowing glances, the weight of tomorrow's journey hanging heavy in the air.

With murmurs of agreement, they rise from their seats, the warmth of familial bonds wrapping around them like a comforting embrace. One by one, they exchange heartfelt goodnights, their voices soft with love and gratitude for the time spent in each other's company.

As Angela, Howard, and their children retreat to their rooms, the house falls quiet, the only sound the gentle whisper of the night breeze through the open windows. And as they drift off to sleep, their dreams are filled with visions of home, family, and the unbreakable bonds that tie them together, no matter the distance.

As the first light of dawn breaks through the curtains, painting the room in soft hues of pink and gold, Howard and Angela begin their morning ritual of preparing for the journey back to Lusaka. Their children, sleepy-eyed but excited, scurry around the room, gathering their belongings and exchanging hugs with their grandparents.

Angela's parents, their faces etched with both pride and reluctance, stand in the doorway, watching as their beloved grandchildren flit about like butterflies preparing to take flight. Howard and Angela exchange knowing glances, their hearts heavy with the bittersweet knowledge that it's time to say goodbye.

With tender embraces and tearful farewells, they gather in the foyer, the air thick with emotion as they prepare to part ways. Angela's parents hold their grandchildren close, reluctant to let go of the precious moments they've shared together.

"Safe travels, my darlings," Angela's mother whispers, her voice trembling with emotion. "We'll miss you terribly."

Howard and Angela exchange one last embrace with their parents, the weight of separation heavy in the air. But as they turn to leave, a glimmer of hope shines through the tears in their eyes – the promise of future reunions and cherished moments yet to come.

With a final wave goodbye, Howard, Angela, and their children step out into the morning sunlight, their hearts filled with love and gratitude for the time spent with family. And as they drive away, the echoes of their laughter and the warmth of their embraces linger in the air, a reminder that no matter the distance, the bonds of love will always keep them close.

As the engine hums to life and the car pulls away from Angela's parents' home, a sense of anticipation fills the air. Howard sits behind the wheel, Angela by his side, their children nestled in the backseat, their chatter and laughter mingling with the soft hum of the road beneath them.

With each passing mile, the landscape unfolds before them like a living tapestry, the colors blending and shifting with the rhythm of their journey. Angela's hand finds Howard's, their fingers intertwining like the threads of fate weaving them together.

The children peer out of the windows, their eyes wide with wonder as they watch the world pass by in a blur of motion and color. They point out landmarks and roadside attractions, their voices filled with excitement and curiosity.

CHAPTER ONE: THE CEO'S FAMILY TIME

As they journey on, the sun climbs higher in the sky, casting long shadows across the road ahead. Angela turns to Howard, a smile playing at the corners of her lips. "Home," she whispers, her voice filled with warmth and anticipation.

Howard nods, his eyes fixed on the horizon. "Home," he echoes, his voice steady and sure. And with that, they continue on their way, their hearts filled with the promise of new adventures and the comfort of familiar surroundings awaiting them in Lusaka.

As the car glides smoothly through the familiar streets of Lusaka, a sense of relief washes over Howard and Angela. The journey, though not long, had felt like an eternity with the anticipation of returning home weighing heavily on their minds.

The children, now weary from the journey, sit quietly in the backseat, their excitement tempered by the fatigue of travel. But as they pass by familiar landmarks and bustling streets, their spirits lift, and smiles begin to grace their tired faces.

Finally, they arrive in Chudleigh, their neighbourhood adorned with blooming jacaranda trees and bustling with the sounds of everyday life. Howard turns onto their street, and a wave of nostalgia washes over him as he takes in the familiar sights and sounds of home.

Angela's eyes light up as they pull into the driveway of their house, the welcoming sight of their home filling her with a sense of warmth and belonging. The children let out cries of joy as they tumble out of the car, eager to explore their surroundings and reunite with their beloved toys and pets.

Howard and Angela exchange a knowing glance, their hearts filled with gratitude for the journey they've taken and the home that awaits them. With a sense of contentment and peace, they step through the front door, ready to embrace the familiar comforts of home and the adventures that await them in the days to come.

As the last rays of sunlight fade into the horizon, casting long shadows across the room, Howard sinks into the depths of his favorite armchair. The silence of the evening envelops him like a heavy cloak, and with it comes the weight of his responsibilities as a CEO.

With a weary sigh, Howard's gaze drifts to the stack of papers on his desk, each one representing a task left unfinished, a decision left unresolved. The reality of his busy schedule looms large in his mind, a constant reminder of the demands placed upon him by his role.

As the world outside grows dark and still, Howard feels the familiar tug of anxiety gnawing at the edges of his consciousness. Meetings to attend, emails to answer, deadlines to meet – the list of tasks seems endless, stretching out before him like an insurmountable mountain.

But amidst the chaos of his thoughts, a small voice whispers of hope – the promise of a new day, filled with fresh opportunities and the chance to make a difference. With renewed determination, Howard rises from his chair, ready to face the challenges that lie ahead.

As he steps out into the cool night air, the stars twinkling overhead like distant beacons of guidance, Howard feels a sense of purpose stir within him. Though the road ahead may be long and difficult, he knows that with perseverance and determination, he will overcome any obstacle in his path.

With the weight of his responsibilities resting heavy upon his shoulders, Howard sets off into the night, ready to conquer whatever challenges the future may hold. For in the darkness, he finds the strength to face the dawn of a new day.

2

Chapter Two: A Glimpse into the CEO's Day's Routine

As the sun begins its ascent, casting a warm glow over the city, Howard strides purposefully into his office, the weight of his responsibilities resting heavy on his shoulders. With each step, the familiar hum of activity fills the air, a symphony of ringing phones and clicking keyboards that signals the start of another busy day.

Summoning his secretary with a quick press of a button, Howard settles into his chair, his mind already racing ahead to the tasks that await him. Moments later, the door swings open, and his secretary enters, a sense of efficiency radiating from her every movement.

"Good morning, Mr. Howard," she greets him with a warm smile, her voice crisp and professional. "I trust you had a restful evening?"

Howard nods, acknowledging her with a grateful smile. "Yes, thank you. Now, what's on the agenda for today?"

The secretary consults her tablet, her fingers flying deftly across the screen as she pulls up Howard's schedule for the day. "Well, sir, you have a series of meetings lined up with depatmental heads and project managers throughout the morning. And this afternoon, you have a conference call with the board of directors to discuss the quarterly financial report."

Howard nods, mentally preparing himself for the day ahead. But before he can delve into his work, the secretary hesitates, a thoughtful expression crossing her face.

"Oh, and there's one more thing, sir," she adds, her tone taking on a note of significance. "Somutech Management Consultants will be conducting a corporate seminar tomorrow on building a 'Strengths-Based Organization.' I believe this is a topic that you've expressed a keen interest in as CEO."

Howard's eyes light up at the mention of the seminar, his passion for organizational development reignited. "Ah, yes, that's right. Thank you for reminding me. Please arrange for the director of Human Resources to join me in my office as soon as possible. I'd like to discuss the details of the program further."

With a nod of understanding, the secretary retreats from the office, leaving Howard to contemplate the opportunities that lie ahead. As he awaits the arrival of the HR director, he feels a surge of excitement at the prospect of shaping the future of his organization. For Howard, the journey towards building a Strengths-Based Organization has only just begun.

As the minutes tick by, the anticipation in the air grows deep, each passing moment bringing Howard closer to the meeting that will shape the future of his organization. Finally, there comes a knock at the door, and without hesitation, Howard calls out, "Come in."

The director of Human Resources steps into the office, his demeanor poised and professional. With a respectful nod, he greets Howard, their eyes meeting in silent understanding of the task that lies before them.

"Good morning, Mr. Howard," the director begins, his voice carrying the weight of the responsibility entrusted to him. "How may I assist you today?"

Howard returns the greeting with a warm smile, gesturing for the director to take a seat. "Thank you for joining me, James," he says, his tone inviting and earnest. "I wanted to bring you up to speed on the upcoming seminar we'll be attending tomorrow."

The director leans forward, his attention fully engaged as Howard outlines the details of the seminar and its importance to the organization. As they delve deeper into the discussion, their shared passion for organizational development becomes apparent, each idea building upon the last with a sense of purpose and clarity.

"It's imperative that we make the most of this opportunity," Howard emphasizes, his voice tinged with determination. "We need to ensure that our organization is positioned to thrive in today's ever-changing business landscape."

The director nods in agreement, his eyes alight with enthusiasm. "Absolutely, sir. I'll make sure everything is in order for our attendance tomorrow. Is there anything specific you'd like me to focus on?"

Howard pauses for a moment, considering his response carefully. "I trust your judgment, James. Just make sure we're prepared to actively participate and engage with the consultants. This seminar could be a game-changer for us, and I want to make sure we're ready to seize the opportunity."

With a firm nod, the director rises from his seat, his resolve evident in every step. "Consider it done, sir. I'll ensure that everything is in place for our attendance tomorrow."

CHAPTER TWO: A GLIMPSE INTO THE CEO'S DAY'S ROUTINE

As the director exits the office, Howard is left alone with his thoughts, a sense of anticipation building within him. Tomorrow's seminar represents more than just an opportunity – it's a chance to shape the future of his organization and set it on a path towards success. And with the director of Human Resources by his side, Howard knows that together, they will rise to meet the challenges that lie ahead.

As the door closes behind the departing director of Human Resources, a hush descends upon the office, punctuated only by the soft click of the latch. Alone now, Howard turns his attention to the task at hand, his mind already shifting gears to focus on the day's impending agenda.

With a determined air, he reaches for the schedule laid out before him, a roadmap to the hours ahead meticulously prepared by his secretary. Each entry on the list represents a commitment, a responsibility waiting to be fulfilled.

As he scans the schedule, his brow furrows in concentration, his thoughts racing ahead to the meetings and decisions that lie ahead. There are emails to answer, reports to review, and decisions to be made – all demanding his attention and expertise.

With a sense of purpose, Howard sets to work, his fingers flying across the keyboard as he responds to emails and drafts memos. Each task is tackled with precision and efficiency, his focus unwavering despite the weight of his responsibilities.

Hours pass in a blur as Howard immerses himself in the demands of his role, his dedication unwavering even in the face of mounting pressure. And as the day wears on, he finds himself buoyed by a sense of accomplishment, each completed task bringing him one step closer to his goals.

But amidst the hustle and bustle of the office, a sense of

anticipation lingers in the air – the promise of tomorrow's seminar, and the opportunity it represents for the future of the organization. With a renewed sense of purpose, Howard redoubles his efforts, determined to make the most of the opportunities that lie ahead.

And as the sun dips below the horizon, casting long shadows across the office, Howard remains at his desk, his resolve unyielding as he prepares for the challenges and triumphs that await him in the days to come.

As the day draws to a close and the office hums with the last-minute flurry of activity, Howard leans back in his chair, his thoughts turning to the week ahead. With a sense of purpose, he reaches for the phone and dials his secretary's number, the urgency in his voice unmistakable.

"Sarah, could you please come to my office? There's something important we need to discuss," he says, his tone firm yet gentle.

Moments later, Sarah steps into the room, a notepad and pen in hand, ready to take down whatever instructions her boss may have for her.

"Sarah, I need you to prepare a diary outlining my schedule for the next two weeks, starting from tomorrow," Howard begins, his voice steady as he lays out his expectations. "I want you to ensure that my family time is prioritized on weekends – no exceptions."

Sarah nods, jotting down notes as Howard continues. "The diary should include our attendance at the Somutech Management Consultant's seminar tomorrow, along with a note for the review of the seminar's presentations with all the directors next week."

Howard pauses, his gaze steady as he meets Sarah's eyes. "I

CHAPTER TWO: A GLIMPSE INTO THE CEO'S DAY'S ROUTINE

need you to ensure that the diary is detailed and comprehensive. This is crucial for our organization's success, and I'm counting on you to make it happen."

Sarah nods, a sense of determination shining in her eyes. "Consider it done, sir. I'll have the diary ready for your approval first thing tomorrow morning."

With a grateful smile, Howard dismisses Sarah, her swift exit marking the end of a long day's work. As he watches her go, a sense of satisfaction washes over him – the first step towards a productive and successful week has been taken, and he knows that with Sarah's help, nothing is impossible.

As the sun begins its descent, casting a warm glow over the city, Howard's mind races with the tasks of the day. But amidst the flurry of responsibilities, there's a gentle reminder from his wife Angela – a request to accompany her and their youngest daughters for a shopping outing at Eastpark Mall.

With a sense of urgency, Howard rushes homeward, his thoughts swirling with anticipation of the time spent with his family. As he pulls into the driveway, his heart swells with love at the sight of Angela and their daughters waiting eagerly by the door, their faces radiant with excitement.

"Welcome home, dear!" Angela exclaims, her voice filled with warmth as she embraces Howard. "We're all set for our shopping trip. Are you ready?"

Howard's fatigue melts away in an instant as he looks upon his family, their enthusiasm infectious. "Absolutely," he replies, a smile spreading across his face. "Let's make it a memorable evening."

Their youngest daughters, their eyes shining with anticipation, chatter excitedly as they pile into the car, their laughter filling the air with joy. With Angela by his side and their daughters in the backseat, Howard feels a sense of completeness wash over him – a reminder of the simple joys that make life worth living.

As they set off for Eastpark Mall, the city lights twinkling in the distance, Howard's heart is full of gratitude for the precious moments shared with his family. And as they embark on their shopping adventure, he knows that no matter where life may take them, they will always find their way back to each other, bound together by love and laughter.

The setting sun casts a golden hue over the city as Howard guides the car homeward, the day's shopping adventures behind them. The car hums with the comforting sound of their journey, but Howard's thoughts are already drifting to the demands of the day ahead.

Turning to his wife, Angela, he sighs softly. "I think I'll turn in early tonight," he says, weariness evident in his voice. "Tomorrow's schedule looks packed, and I need to be at my best."

Angela nods in understanding, her own fatigue mirroring his. "Of course, dear," she replies, her voice filled with warmth and concern. "I'll make sure you get the rest you need."

Back at home, the familiar sights and sounds envelop them like a warm embrace. Their son Tony, ever the eager sports fan, reminds his father of the evening's EPL soccer match. But Howard's heart sinks as he realizes that his responsibilities will once again keep him from enjoying a simple pleasure with his family.

"I'm sorry, Tony," he says, a hint of regret in his voice. "I won't be able to watch the match tonight. But we'll catch the next one together, I promise."

After a soothing hot bath that washes away the cares of the

day, Howard joins Angela and their children at the dinner table. The aroma of Angela's cooking fills the air, comforting and inviting.

As they eat, laughter and conversation fill the room, momentarily lifting the weight of their responsibilities. But as dinner draws to a close, Howard feels the fatigue of the day settling over him once more.

Angela looks at him with a soft smile. "Are you ready to turn in, love?" she asks gently.

Howard nods, grateful for her understanding and support. "Yes, thank you," he replies, rising from the table and bidding goodnight to their children. With a final glance back at his family, he makes his way to their bedroom, the promise of a peaceful night's sleep calling to him.

As he settles beneath the covers, surrounded by the quiet of their home, Howard feels a sense of gratitude wash over him. Tomorrow may bring its challenges, but for now, he is content to rest in the love and warmth of his family, knowing that they are his greatest source of strength.

As the first light of dawn filters through the curtains on a Tuesday morning, casting a soft glow over the room, Angela gently shakes Howard awake. He stirs, blinking away the remnants of sleep, and as consciousness slowly returns, he becomes aware of Angela's gentle voice beside him.

"Good morning, dear," she says, her voice infused with warmth and encouragement. "It's time to wake up and prepare for the busy day ahead."

Howard rubs his eyes, the weight of sleep still heavy upon him. But Angela's reminder serves as a gentle nudge, urging him to shake off the remnants of slumber and face the day with determination.

With a sigh, he nods in acknowledgment, his mind already beginning to churn with thoughts of the tasks that await him. The day ahead promises to be demanding, filled with meetings, decisions, and responsibilities that cannot be ignored.

But as he rises from the warmth of his bed, Angela's presence beside him serves as a source of strength and motivation. Her unwavering support is a reminder that he is not alone in facing the challenges of the day – together, they will navigate the stormy waters ahead.

With a grateful smile, Howard begins to prepare himself for the day, his mind focused and his spirit determined. Morning has dawned, and with it comes the promise of new opportunities and fresh beginnings. And as he sets out to meet the challenges that lie ahead, Angela's words echo in his mind, filling him with the courage to tackle whatever the day may bring.

With a sense of purpose driving him forward, Howard steps out into the crisp morning air, the weight of responsibility resting squarely on his shoulders. Each step towards his office is deliberate, each breath a reminder of the challenges that lie ahead.

As he crosses the threshold into his workspace, a wave of familiarity washes over him, grounding him in the present moment. With a determined stride, he settles into his chair, the desk before him a battlefield awaiting his command.

Without wasting a moment, he reaches for the intercom, summoning his secretary with a sense of urgency. Moments later, there's a soft knock at the door, and she enters, a vision of efficiency and professionalism.

"Good morning, Mr. Howard," she greets him, her voice a symphony of deference and respect. "You called for the diary?"

CHAPTER TWO: A GLIMPSE INTO THE CEO'S DAY'S ROUTINE

Howard nods, his gaze fixed on the task at hand. "Yes, please," he replies, his tone steady and unwavering. "I need to have a clear understanding of the week ahead."

With practiced ease, his secretary places the diary before him, her fingers gliding over the pages with precision and grace. As she orients him through the schedule, Howard listens intently, his mind absorbing the details with razor-sharp focus.

Each entry in the diary is a puzzle piece, a glimpse into the intricate tapestry of his week ahead. Meetings, appointments, deadlines – each one a challenge waiting to be conquered, each one an opportunity to prove his mettle as a leader.

With each passing moment, Howard's determination grows, fueled by the knowledge that success is within his grasp. As his secretary concludes her briefing, he nods in gratitude, a sense of purpose burning bright in his eyes.

Armed with the knowledge of the week ahead, Howard is ready to face whatever challenges come his way. With a resolute spirit and a steady hand, he sets off to conquer the day, knowing that with careful planning and unwavering determination, there is nothing he cannot achieve.

The CEO and his esteemed Director of Human Resources embark on a journey of knowledge and enlightenment. At the stroke of 9:00 AM, they grace the Somutech Management Consultants seminar with their presence, poised to immerse themselves in the wealth of wisdom that awaits.

In the hallowed halls of academia, minds collide and ideas flourish as the seminar unfolds. The hours slip away unnoticed, punctuated only by the chiming of the clock as it strikes noon, granting a brief respite for sustenance and reflection.

Rejuvenated by the repast, the CEO and his director return to the seminar, where the afternoon session awaits. With each passing hour, the depth of their understanding deepens, fueled by the passion for knowledge that burns within their souls.

As the day draws to a close, the seminar concludes with a flourish, leaving the CEO and his director enriched and enlightened. But their work is far from over. As the clock strikes 5:00 PM, they retreat to the sanctum of their offices, where they diligently review the materials gathered throughout the day.

With a meticulous eye for detail and a commitment to excellence, they pore over each document, extracting insights and formulating strategies for the challenges that lie ahead. In this sacred space of collaboration and dedication, the CEO and his director work in harmony, their shared vision propelling them ever closer to their goals.

And as the evening shadows lengthen and the world outside grows still, they emerge from their chambers, fortified and ready to face whatever tomorrow may bring, confident in the knowledge that they are prepared for whatever challenges lie ahead.

With the dawn of a new day, the CEO and the Director of Human Resources embark upon the next chapter of their journey at the esteemed Somutech Management Consultants seminar, where the theme of "Building a Strength Based Organization" takes center stage. At precisely 9:00 AM, they arrive at the venue, their hearts brimming with anticipation and their minds primed for the wealth of knowledge that awaits.

Within the hallowed halls of the seminar venue, the atmosphere crackles with intellectual energy as participants engage in dynamic discussions and thought-provoking presentations. The CEO and the Director immerse themselves fully in the proceedings, their eyes alight with the spark of inspiration as they absorb each insightful nugget of wisdom.

As the clock strikes noon, the seminar breaks for lunch, providing a moment of respite amidst the intellectual intensity. Amidst the clatter of cutlery and the buzz of conversation, the CEO and the Director take the opportunity to refuel their bodies and minds, nourishing themselves for the journey that lies ahead.

At 1:00 PM, they return to the seminar hall, ready to delve deeper into the exploration of strength-based organizational principles. The afternoon session unfolds with a symphony of ideas and insights, each revelation adding another layer to their understanding of the intricate tapestry of organizational dynamics.

As the sun begins its graceful descent towards the horizon, casting a warm glow over the horizon, the seminar draws to a close at 4:00 PM. With hearts enriched and minds expanded, the CEO and the Director bid farewell to their fellow participants, grateful for the opportunity to have been a part of such a transformative experience.

But the day's work is far from over. As evening descends and the world grows quiet, the CEO and the Director retreat to the sanctuary of their offices, where they diligently review the seminar materials. With meticulous attention to detail, they analyze, synthesize, and strategize, laying the groundwork for the challenges that tomorrow may bring.

In this sacred space of reflection and preparation, the CEO and the Director work in harmony, their shared vision guiding them towards the path of organizational excellence. And as the clock strikes 5:00 PM, they emerge from their chambers, fortified and ready to face whatever the future may hold, confident in their ability to lead their organization to new heights of success.

In the sanctum of his office, the CEO and his trusted Director engage in a solemn discussion, their voices hushed in anticipation of the momentous task that lies ahead. With a flicker of determination in his eyes, the CEO leans forward, his gaze fixed upon his colleague as they chart the course for the days to come.

"We must ensure that tomorrow's discussion and brainstorming session is nothing short of exceptional," the CEO declares, his words ringing with authority and conviction. "The seminar report holds the key to our organization's future, and it is imperative that we approach it with the utmost care and diligence."

His Director nods in agreement, a steely resolve mirrored in his own countenance. "Indeed," he responds, his voice steady and resolute. "We must delve deep into the heart of the report, extracting every ounce of insight and wisdom it has to offer. Only then can we unlock the full potential of our organization."

With a sense of purpose guiding their every move, the CEO and his Director begin to map out their strategy for the upcoming discussion. They outline the key topics to be addressed, the questions to be asked, and the goals to be achieved, their minds ablaze with the possibilities that lie before them.

As they delve deeper into their plans, a sense of excitement fills the room, buoyed by the knowledge that they are on the brink of something truly extraordinary. With hearts united and minds aligned, they vow to approach tomorrow's meeting with unwavering focus and determination, knowing that together, they possess the power to shape the destiny of their organization.

And as they conclude their discussion, a quiet sense of anticipation hangs in the air, a silent promise of the greatness that is yet to come. For tomorrow, as Thursday dawns, they will gather with their fellow directors, ready to embark upon a journey of exploration and discovery, united in their quest to propel their organization to new heights of success.

3

Chapter Three: Introduction to Strength-Based Organizations

On a crisp Friday morning, the CEO's footsteps echo through the corridors of power as he strides purposefully towards the boardroom. His presence commands attention, a silent signal that something of importance is about to transpire.

As the clock strikes 9:00 AM, the directors - each representing a different facet of the organization's multifaceted operations - assemble in the hallowed confines of the boardroom. Their faces are a tapestry of anticipation and curiosity, each one eager to glean insights from the impending deliberations.

The CEO enters the room, his demeanor radiating authority and gravitas. With a nod of acknowledgment, he greets each director in turn, recognizing their invaluable contributions to the organization. The exchange of formalities is brief but respectful, a prelude to the weighty discussions that lie ahead.

With the pleasantries concluded, the CEO wastes no time in setting the agenda for the meeting. His voice is steady and commanding as he outlines the objectives and expectations for the deliberations. Each director - from finance to operations, marketing to technology - listens intently, poised to offer their expertise and insights.

But one seat remains conspicuously empty - that of the Director of Human Resources. The CEO's gaze lingers momentarily on the vacant chair, a silent acknowledgment of its significance in shaping the organization's most valuable asset - its people.

With the stage set and the players assembled, the CEO gestures for the meeting to commence. The air crackles with anticipation as the directors lean forward, ready to engage in the spirited exchange of ideas and strategies that will shape the future of the organization.

And so, with the formalities observed and the agenda set, the CEO and his cadre of directors embark on a journey of discovery and innovation, united in their quest to chart a course towards greatness.

As the CEO prepares to address the gathered directors, a hush falls over the room, anticipation thick in the air like a tangible presence. His hand hovers over the documents before him, poised to unveil the subject matter that will shape the course of their discussions.

But just as he is about to speak, the door swings open with a soft click, and all heads turn as one to behold the figure standing in the threshold. It is the Director of Human Resources, his expression apologetic as he steps into the room.

"I apologize for my tardiness," he begins, his voice contrite yet determined. "An unforeseen circumstance delayed my arrival, but I am fully committed to participating in today's discussions."

The CEO's gaze softens with understanding, a silent acknowledgment of the challenges that can arise in the daily hustle and bustle of corporate life. With a nod of acceptance, he gestures for the Director of Human Resources to take his seat, signaling the continuation of the meeting.

As the Director settles into his chair, a sense of unity washes over the room, bridging the gap that momentarily threatened to divide them. With everyone present and accounted for, the CEO resumes his position at the head of the table, ready to guide the proceedings with wisdom and grace.

And so, with the Director of Human Resources welcomed into the fold, the meeting presses forward, fueled by a renewed sense of purpose and camaraderie. For in the crucible of collaboration, even the most unexpected twists and turns can become opportunities for growth and unity.

With a commanding presence, the CEO stands at the head of the boardroom table, his gaze sweeping across the assembled team members. The air crackles with anticipation as he prepares to share the insights gleaned from the recent seminar.

"My esteemed colleagues," he begins, his voice resonating with authority, "I am eager to bring you up to speed on the seminar that the Director of Human Resources and I had the privilege of attending."

As he speaks, the CEO's words carry a weight of importance, each syllable carefully chosen to convey the gravity of the subject matter. "The theme of the seminar," he continues, "was 'Building a Strengths-Based Organization.'"

A ripple of intrigue courses through the room at the mention of the theme, curiosity etched on the faces of the team members. Sensing their interest, the CEO leans forward, his expression earnest as he elaborates on the significance of the topic.

After the introductions are made, the CEO stands tall, commanding the attention of the room. With a confident demeanor, he begins to delve into the intricacies of the topic at hand, "Understanding the Strength-Based Approach."

He gestures towards the projector screen, where a series of slides illuminate the room with key concepts and insights. "Ladies and gentlemen," he begins, his voice resonating with authority, "today, we embark on a journey to uncover the transformative power of leveraging our strengths."

As he speaks, his words are infused with passion and conviction, each sentence carefully crafted to convey the importance of embracing a strengths-based approach. "Too often," he explains, "we focus on our weaknesses, striving to overcome them at the expense of neglecting our inherent strengths."

His eyes scan the room, locking onto each member of the audience with unwavering intensity. "But imagine," he continues, his voice rising with enthusiasm, "what we could achieve if we shifted our perspective. What if we recognized and celebrated our strengths, harnessing them to drive innovation, productivity, and success?"

With each passing moment, the CEO's words resonate deeply with his audience, igniting a spark of curiosity and inspiration within them. He illustrates his points with real-life examples, weaving a narrative that captivates the minds and hearts of those in attendance.

"Our strengths are not just individual attributes," he declares, his voice reverberating with conviction. "They are the foundation upon which we build our organizations, our teams, and our futures."

"Building a Strengths-Based Organization," he explains, "is not merely a catchphrase, but a fundamental shift in our approach to leadership and management. It is about recognizing and leveraging the unique talents and abilities of each team member to drive organizational success."

His words hang in the air, each member of the team absorbing the gravity of the concept. The CEO's passion for the subject is evident in his delivery, his eyes alight with fervor as he imparts his knowledge to his eager audience.

"As we embark on this journey together," he concludes, "let us embrace the principles of a strengths-based approach, empowering each other to reach new heights of excellence. Together, we will chart a course towards a future filled with limitless possibilities."

With that, the CEO concludes his introduction, leaving the team inspired and invigorated by the vision he has set forth. As they nod in agreement, a sense of unity washes over the room, binding them together in their shared commitment to building a strengths-based organization worthy of admiration and success.

As the CEO leans forward, the room falls silent, every eye fixed on him with unwavering attention. With a sense of purpose, he begins to unravel the intricacies of what it truly means to build a Strengths-Based Organization.

"My esteemed colleagues," he begins, his voice carrying the weight of conviction, "let us delve into the essence of what it means to embrace a Strengths-Based Organization."

His words hang in the air, a palpable anticipation building among the team members as they wait for him to illuminate the path forward.

"Building a Strengths-Based Organization," the CEO continues, his tone resonant with authority, "is not merely about acknowledging the talents of our team members. It is about harnessing those talents to propel our organization towards excellence."

He pauses, allowing his words to sink in, the gravity of his message settling over the room like a heavy blanket. "It is about fostering an environment where each individual feels empowered to leverage their strengths to achieve shared goals. It's about recognizing that our collective success is built upon the unique contributions of each and every team member."

With each word, the CEO paints a vivid picture of what a Strengths-Based Organization entails. He speaks of collaboration, innovation, and a shared sense of purpose, weaving together the threads of inspiration that will guide their journey forward.

"As we embark on this journey together," he concludes, his voice ringing with determination, "let us embrace the principles of a Strengths-Based Organization with unwavering commitment and resolve. For it is through the collective harnessing of our strengths that we will achieve greatness."

With that, the CEO concludes his address, leaving the team members stirred by the passion and vision he has imparted. As they nod in agreement, a renewed sense of purpose fills the room, binding them together in their shared mission to build a Strengths-Based Organization that will stand the test of time.

As the CEO concludes his impassioned address, a collective sense of determination fills the room, each team member inspired by the vision he has laid out before them. With a nod of acknowledgment, the CEO gestures for a brief recess, allowing the team to gather their thoughts and recharge for the discussions ahead.

As the clock strikes 10:30 AM, the room empties as team members file out into the hallway, their conversations animated with excitement and anticipation. The atmosphere is alive with energy, the promise of progress lingering in the air like a tangible presence.

In the break room, the aroma of freshly brewed coffee and tea fills the air, mingling with the sounds of laughter and friendship. Team members gather around the refreshments, exchanging stories and sharing insights, each moment of respite a chance to bond and connect.

As the minutes tick by, the CEO joins his colleagues, a warm smile on his face as he engages in light-hearted conversation. Despite the weighty topics that await them, there is a sense of friendship among the team, a shared understanding that they are in this together.

At precisely 12:00 PM, the CEO rises from his seat, signaling the end of the break. With a sense of purpose, the team members begin to make their way back to the boardroom, their minds focused and their spirits renewed.

As they settle back into their seats, the room once again falls silent, the energy crackling with anticipation for the discussions to come. With refreshed minds and invigorated spirits, the team is ready to resume their meeting, united in their mission to build a Strengths-Based Organization that will redefine the future of their company.

As the clock strikes noon, the team reconvenes in the boardroom, their minds still abuzz with the CEO's earlier revelations. The air is charged with anticipation as they settle into their seats, ready to delve deeper into the concept of building a Strengths-Based Organization.

With a nod from the CEO, the discussion resumes, the room alive with the hum of animated conversation. The CEO takes the lead once more, his voice steady and resolute as he guides the team through the intricacies of the Strengths-Based Approach.

CHAPTER THREE: INTRODUCTION TO STRENGTH-BASED ORGANIZATIONS

"Let us continue our exploration of the Strengths-Based Approach," he begins, his words carrying a weight of importance. "As we discussed earlier, it is not enough to simply acknowledge the talents of our team members. We must actively work to create an environment that nurtures and celebrates those talents."

The team listens intently, hanging on his every word as he outlines the need for a cultural shift within the organization. "We must move away from a mindset focused solely on weaknesses," he explains, his tone earnest. "Instead, we must embrace a culture that encourages individuals to leverage their strengths to achieve their full potential."

As they discuss over lunch, the CEO emphasizes the importance of fostering a sense of belonging and empowerment among employees. "We must create opportunities for growth and development," he continues, "and provide the support and encouragement needed for individuals to thrive."

The team nods in agreement, each member recognizing the significance of their role in driving this cultural shift. Ideas flow freely as they brainstorm ways to create an environment that nurtures and celebrates employee talents, their enthusiasm palpable in the air.

The CEO, refusing to take a seat, maintains a commanding presence in the room. With a fervent energy, he delves deeper into the topic at hand, "Understanding the Strength-Based Approach."

His stance exudes confidence as he paces back and forth, his gestures punctuating each point with emphasis. "Let's explore this further," he declares, his voice resonating with authority. "The strength-based approach isn't just a strategy—it's a mindset, a philosophy that shapes our entire organizational culture."

His eyes scan the room, locking onto each individual with unwavering intensity. "We must shift our focus," he urges, "from fixing weaknesses to maximizing strengths. That's where true potential lies."

As he speaks, his words paint a vivid picture of possibility, igniting a spark of inspiration within his audience. He shares anecdotes and examples, illustrating the transformative power of leveraging strengths in both personal and professional contexts.

"We have untapped potential within us," he continues, his voice rising with passion. "It's time to unlock it, to embrace it fully and harness it for the greater good of our organization."

The CEO's words resonate deeply, stirring something within each person present. They lean forward, hanging on his every word, captivated by his vision for a strengths-driven future.

With each passing moment, the CEO's conviction grows stronger, his belief in the strength-based approach unwavering. "Together," he concludes, his voice ringing out with determination, "we can chart a new course—one defined by empowerment, innovation, and unparalleled success."

As he finally takes a seat, the room erupts into applause, filled with a renewed sense of purpose and possibility. The CEO's impassioned words have ignited a flame of inspiration, setting the stage for a transformative journey ahead.

As the CEO finishes his explanation on "Understanding the Strength-Based Approach," he opens the floor for questions, eager to engage with his directors and address any lingering doubts or inquiries.

Director Smith, known for his analytical mind, raises his hand first. "How do we ensure that we accurately identify and leverage each individual's strengths within our organization?"

CHAPTER THREE: INTRODUCTION TO STRENGTH-BASED ORGANIZATIONS

he queries, his brow furrowed with curiosity.

The CEO nods thoughtfully before responding, "Excellent question, Smith. It begins with comprehensive assessments and ongoing feedback loops. We need to utilize tools like strengths assessments and performance reviews to pinpoint strengths and provide opportunities for their development."

Director Rodriguez, known for her strategic thinking, follows up with her question. "How can we align individual strengths with the broader goals and objectives of our organization?" she asks, her voice poised and confident.

The CEO smiles, recognizing the importance of strategic alignment. "That's a crucial aspect, Rodriguez," he replies. "We must foster a culture of transparency and collaboration, ensuring that individuals understand how their strengths contribute to the organization's overall success. This requires clear communication and strategic planning to maximize synergy."

Lastly, Director Chen, renowned for her focus on employee well-being, poses her question. "How can we support employees in recognizing and embracing their strengths, especially in times of change or uncertainty?" she inquires, her concern evident in her tone.

The CEO nods empathetically, acknowledging the significance of employee support. "Indeed, Chen," he responds warmly. "We must prioritize ongoing training and development, coupled with consistent feedback and mentorship opportunities. Additionally, fostering a culture of psychological safety and resilience is paramount to empowering individuals to embrace their strengths, even in challenging circumstances."

With each question addressed, the room buzzes with renewed clarity and understanding. The CEO's insightful responses have not only quelled any lingering uncertainties but have also inspired a deeper appreciation for the power of a strength-based approach within the organization.

With each passing moment, the vision of a Strengths-Based Organization becomes clearer, its promise of empowerment and innovation lighting the way forward. And as they break for lunch, the team is filled with renewed determination to turn this vision into reality.

As the team filters back into the boardroom at 3:00 PM after the lunch break, the atmosphere crackles with anticipation. The CEO stands at the head of the table, his presence commanding attention as he prepares to address the group once more.

Without wasting a moment, he launches into his explanation, his words carrying a sense of urgency and purpose. "My esteemed colleagues," he begins, his voice resonating with conviction, "it's time we delve deeper into why strengths matter in Organizational Development."

The room falls silent as the CEO begins to unravel the intricacies of the topic. With each word, he paints a vivid picture of the transformative power of embracing strengths within an organization.

"Strengths are not just individual attributes," he explains, his eyes alight with fervor. "They are the building blocks of success, the key to unlocking the full potential of our organization."

He pauses, allowing his words to sink in, the gravity of his message settling over the room like a heavy blanket. "When we leverage the strengths of our team members," he continues, "we create a culture of empowerment and innovation. We foster collaboration and creativity, driving our organization towards new heights of excellence."

CHAPTER THREE: INTRODUCTION TO STRENGTH-BASED ORGANIZATIONS

The team listens intently, hanging on his every word as he illustrates the profound impact that a strengths-based approach can have on Organizational Development.

"With each individual empowered to harness their strengths," he concludes, his voice ringing with determination, "we create a ripple effect of success that permeates every aspect of our organization. It's time we embrace the power of strengths and unlock the limitless potential that lies within each and every one of us."

With that, the CEO concludes his explanation, leaving the team inspired and invigorated by the vision he has set forth. As they nod in agreement, a renewed sense of purpose fills the room, propelling them forward on their collective journey towards building a stronger, more resilient organization.

As the day draws to a close, the CEO continues to elucidate the matter further, his gaze sweeping across the room with a sense of purpose. The team watches him intently, their anticipation profound as they await his final words of wisdom.

"My esteemed colleagues," he continues, his voice commanding attention, "as we bring today's discussions to a close, I want to thank each and every one of you for your unwavering dedication and insight."

The room falls silent, a moment of reverence for the journey they have embarked upon together. With a nod of acknowledgment, the CEO continues, his words carrying the weight of their collective vision.

"But our work is far from over," he declares, his tone resolute. "We must now turn our attention to embedding strength-based leadership practices into our organizational culture."

The team leans in, eager to hear his guidance on the next steps of their journey. With a flourish, the CEO outlines a plan for action, his words igniting a spark of inspiration in the hearts of his listeners.

"We must identify key areas for further exploration," he continues, his voice steady and unwavering. "This includes implementing training programs to equip our team members with the tools they need to lead with strength and integrity."

The team nods in agreement, recognizing the importance of investing in their own development as leaders. But the CEO is not finished yet. With a gleam in his eye, he reveals his final strategy for success.

"We must also prioritize communication initiatives," he asserts, his words echoing with determination. "It is through open and transparent communication that we will foster a culture of trust and collaboration, enabling us to truly thrive as an organization."

As the team absorbs his words, a sense of excitement fills the room. They are ready to embrace the challenges and opportunities that lie ahead, united in their shared commitment to building a stronger, more resilient organization.

As the topic of "Why Strengths Matter in Organizational Development" takes center stage, the directors eagerly prepare their questions, poised to delve deeper into the subject.

Director Smith, known for his analytical prowess, raises his hand first. "How do strengths contribute to employee engagement and retention?" he queries, his voice carrying a hint of skepticism.

The CEO nods, acknowledging the importance of this inquiry. "Great question, Smith," he responds, his tone confident yet approachable. "Strengths play a crucial role in fostering employee engagement by aligning individuals with tasks that resonate with their innate talents. When employees feel valued for their strengths, they are more likely to be engaged and committed to their roles, leading to higher retention rates."

Director Rodriguez, renowned for her strategic thinking, follows up with her question. "How can strengths-based approaches enhance team dynamics and collaboration?" she asks, her gaze focused and attentive.

The CEO smiles, recognizing the significance of team synergy. "Excellent question, Rodriguez," he replies, his demeanor poised and articulate. "Strengths-based approaches promote a deeper understanding of team dynamics by leveraging each member's unique strengths. By recognizing and harnessing these strengths, teams can optimize collaboration, capitalize on complementary skills, and achieve greater cohesion and productivity."

Lastly, Director Chen, known for her emphasis on employee well-being, poses her question. "In what ways do strengths contribute to individual and organizational resilience, particularly during times of change or adversity?" she inquires, her tone reflecting genuine concern.

The CEO nods empathetically, acknowledging the importance of resilience. "An insightful question, Chen," he responds warmly, his expression conveying empathy and understanding. "Strengths provide a solid foundation for both individual and organizational resilience. By focusing on what individuals do best, even in challenging circumstances, strengths-based approaches empower employees to navigate change with confidence and adaptability, ultimately fostering a resilient organizational culture."

With each question addressed, the room buzzes with renewed insight and understanding. The CEO's thoughtful responses have not only shed light on the importance of strengths in organizational development but have also sparked a deeper appreciation for their transformative potential within the workplace.

As the final rays of sunlight filter through the windows of the boardroom, casting long shadows across the table, the CEO rises from his seat with a sense of accomplishment. His gaze sweeps across the room, lingering on each member of the team with a nod of acknowledgment.

"My esteemed colleagues," he states, his voice resonating with warmth and gratitude, "it has been a day filled with meaningful discussions and valuable insights. I want to thank each and every one of you for your dedication and commitment."

The team members exchange smiles and nods, their faces illuminated by the soft glow of the setting sun. They have worked tirelessly throughout the day, united in their shared pursuit of excellence.

"But now," the CEO continues, "it is time to disperse and rest, for tomorrow will bring new challenges and opportunities. Let us carry forward the momentum of today's discussions as we continue on our journey towards building a stronger, more resilient organization."

With a final nod of farewell, the CEO bids his team goodnight, watching as they gather their belongings and begin to make their way out of the boardroom. There is a sense of camaraderie in the air, a shared understanding of the importance of the work they have accomplished together.

As the last team member exits the room, the CEO lingers for a moment, reflecting on the day's events with a sense of satisfaction. Tomorrow may bring new challenges, but he is confident that together, they will overcome them, stronger and more united than ever before. With a smile of determination, he switches off the lights and closes the door behind him, ready to face whatever the future may hold.

As the team begins to disperse from the boardroom, the Director of Operations steps forward, his demeanor respectful yet determined. With a slight clearing of his throat, he catches the CEO's attention.

"Excuse me, sir," he begins, his tone deferential, "may I make a suggestion for tomorrow's meeting?"

The CEO turns to face him, curiosity flickering in his eyes. "Of course, James," he replies, inviting the director to continue.

James straightens his posture, gathering his thoughts before speaking. "I believe it would be beneficial for us to use a PowerPoint presentation during tomorrow's meeting," he proposes. "It would help to visually illustrate our points and keep the team engaged."

The CEO considers the suggestion for a moment before nodding in agreement. "That's a great idea, James," he acknowledges with a smile. "Let's plan to incorporate that into our presentation tomorrow."

However, before James can respond, the CEO continues with a surprising announcement. "And speaking of the presentation, James," he adds, "I think it's only fitting that you lead it tomorrow. You have a deep understanding of the material, and I trust you to deliver it with confidence and clarity."

James blinks in surprise, caught off guard by the unexpected turn of events. "Thank you, sir," he manages to reply, his voice tinged with gratitude.

With a reassuring smile, the CEO turns to the secretary, who has been quietly observing the exchange. "Sarah," he addresses her, "please ensure that the presentation equipment is ready for tomorrow's meeting. We'll be using it for the remainder of our discussions."

Sarah nods in acknowledgment, jotting down a quick note in her planner. "Of course, sir," she confirms with a warm smile.

As the CEO and his team go their separate ways, there's a sense of excitement in the air. Tomorrow's meeting promises to be an opportunity for James to shine, and the entire team is eager to see the results of their collective efforts come to fruition. With renewed determination, they prepare to tackle whatever challenges lie ahead, confident in their ability to succeed together.

As the team begins to disperse from the boardroom, the Director of Human Resources steps forward, his demeanor respectful yet determined. With a slight clearing of his throat, he catches the CEO's attention.

"Excuse me, sir," he begins, his tone deferential, "may I make a suggestion for tomorrow's meeting?"

The CEO turns to face him, curiosity flickering in his eyes. "Of course, James," he replies, inviting the director to continue.

James straightens his posture, gathering his thoughts before speaking. "I believe it would be beneficial for us to use a PowerPoint presentation during tomorrow's meeting," he proposes. "It would help to visually illustrate our points and keep the team engaged."

The CEO considers the suggestion for a moment before nodding in agreement. "That's a great idea, James," he acknowledges with a smile. "Let's plan to incorporate that into our presentation tomorrow."

However, before James can respond, the CEO continues with a surprising announcement. "And speaking of the presentation, James," he adds, "I think it's only fitting that you lead it tomorrow. You have a deep understanding of the material,

CHAPTER THREE: INTRODUCTION TO STRENGTH-BASED ORGANIZATIONS

and I trust you to deliver it with confidence and clarity."

James blinks in surprise, caught off guard by the unexpected turn of events. "Thank you, sir," he manages to reply, his voice tinged with gratitude.

With a reassuring smile, the CEO turns to the secretary, who has been quietly observing the exchange. "Sarah," he addresses her, "please ensure that the presentation equipment is ready for tomorrow's meeting. We'll be using it for the remainder of our discussions."

Sarah nods in acknowledgment, jotting down a quick note in her planner. "Of course, sir," she confirms with a warm smile.

As the CEO and his team go their separate ways, there's a sense of excitement in the air. Tomorrow's meeting promises to be an opportunity for James to shine, and the entire team is eager to see the results of their collective efforts come to fruition. With renewed determination, they prepare to tackle whatever challenges lie ahead, confident in their ability to succeed together.

4

Chapter Four: The Foundation of Strength-Based Leadership

As the soft light of Friday morning filters through the windows of the boardroom, illuminating the polished surfaces and casting a warm glow over the room, the CEO stands at the head of the table, exuding an aura of quiet authority and confidence. With a welcoming smile, he greets each member of the team as they enter the room, their footsteps echoing softly on the pristine floors.

"Good morning, everyone," he begins, his voice resonating with warmth and energy. "I hope you all had a restful evening and are ready to tackle the day ahead."

The team members nod in agreement, their expressions a mixture of determination and anticipation. There's a sense of purpose in the air, a tangible excitement for the work that lies ahead.

With a graceful gesture, the CEO invites everyone to take their seats, his presence commanding attention as he prepares to lead them through another day of important discussions and decisions.

CHAPTER FOUR: THE FOUNDATION OF STRENGTH-BASED LEADERSHIP

"Today marks the beginning of our second day of meetings," he continues, his tone filled with determination. "And I have no doubt that together, we will continue to make great progress towards our goals."

As the team settles into their seats, the CEO's words hang in the air, a rallying cry for unity and collaboration. With a renewed sense of purpose, they prepare to dive into the day's agenda, ready to tackle whatever challenges may come their way.

As clock strikes 9:00 AM, the CEO gracefully passes the torch to James, the Director of Human Resources, the room buzzes with anticipation. James stands tall, a sense of purpose emanating from his every movement as he steps into the spotlight.

"Thank you, sir," James begins, his voice steady and assured. "Let's delve deeper into the essence of Strength-Based Leadership."

As James leans back in his chair, he clears his throat, preparing to address the eager faces gathered around the conference table. With a dramatic pause, he begins, "Gentlemen, ladies, today we embark on a journey that will redefine the very essence of leadership within our organization." Pointing to the first item on the agenda, he declared with fervor, "Introduction! A critical foundation in any organizational context.

We're not merely talking about leadership; we're talking about a seismic shift towards Strength-Based Leadership!" The room buzzed with anticipation as James continued, his voice rising with passion, "Understanding Strength-Based Leadership is paramount.

It's about more than just words on a page; it's about redefining our approach to individual and team dynamics!

"Definition," he exclaims, leaning forward for emphasis, "We're talking about harnessing the raw power of individual and team strengths! No more dwelling on weaknesses; it's time to embrace the positive forces that drive us forward!"

With a sweeping gesture, James delves into the key characteristics of Strength-Based Leadership, his eyes alight with intensity. "Focus on Development and Growth! Recognition and Utilization of Strengths! Inspiring and Motivating Others! Promoting Collaboration and Inclusivity! These are not just ideals; they are the very pillars upon which our future success rests!"

"But wait, there's more!" James declares, a glint of determination in his eyes. "Principles of Strength-Based Leadership! Building on Strengths, not fixating on weaknesses! Creating a Culture of Trust and Psychological Safety! Embracing Diversity and Inclusion! Encouraging Innovation and Adaptability! These principles aren't just guidelines; they're our roadmap to greatness!"

As murmurs of agreement filled the room, James presses on, undeterred. "Benefits of Strength-Based Leadership! Enhanced Employee Engagement and Satisfaction! Improved Team Performance and Collaboration! Higher Levels of Innovation and Creativity! Increased Organizational Resilience and Agility! These aren't just promises; they're the rewards of our collective efforts!"

"Now, my friends," James declares, his voice ringing with conviction, "Implementing Strength-Based Leadership! Assessing and Developing Individual and Team Strengths! Aligning Organizational Goals with Employee Strengths! Providing Feedback and Recognition Based on Strengths! Modeling Strength-Based Behaviors as a Leader! These actions aren't

CHAPTER FOUR: THE FOUNDATION OF STRENGTH-BASED LEADERSHIP

just tasks; they're the building blocks of our future success!"

As the room erupts into applause, James raises his hand for silence. "But let us not forget the challenges that lie ahead," he cautions, his tone somber yet resolute. "Overcoming Resistance to Change! Addressing Potential Pitfalls and Limitations! Ensuring Alignment with Organizational Culture and Values! These obstacles aren't roadblocks; they're opportunities for growth!"

With a final flourish, James concludes, "In conclusion, my friends, let us recap the principles of Strength-Based Leadership. Let us heed the call to action and embrace Strength-Based Approaches with unwavering determination. For the future of our organization, and indeed, the future of leadership itself, rests in our hands!"

As the director concludes his insightful discourse on "Defining Strength-Based Leadership," the directors eagerly prepare to engage with their questions, eager to glean further understanding from James, the esteemed speaker.

Director Smith, renowned for his probing inquiries, raises his hand first. "How does strength-based leadership differ from traditional leadership approaches?" he asks, his tone reflecting a blend of curiosity and analytical acumen.

James nods thoughtfully, acknowledging the significance of Smith's question. "An excellent point, Smith," he responds, his voice resonating with confidence and clarity. "Strength-based leadership differs from traditional approaches by focusing on identifying and leveraging the unique strengths of individuals. Rather than attempting to mold employees to fit preconceived notions of leadership, strength-based leaders empower their team members to excel in areas where they naturally thrive."

Director Rodriguez, known for her strategic insights, follows up with her question. "Can you provide examples of how strength-based leadership has been successfully implemented in organizations?" she inquires, her gaze steady and intent.

James smiles, recognizing the relevance of Rodriguez's query. "A compelling question, Rodriguez," he replies, his demeanor poised and engaging. "Strength-based leadership has been successfully implemented in various organizations, from startups to multinational corporations. For instance, companies like Google and Deloitte have embraced strength-based approaches in their leadership development programs, resulting in increased employee engagement, productivity, and overall organizational success."

Director Chen, with her emphasis on employee well-being, poses her question next. "How can strength-based leadership contribute to fostering a positive organizational culture?" she asks, her tone reflecting genuine concern for the welfare of employees.

James nods empathetically, acknowledging the importance of Chen's inquiry. "A thoughtful question, Chen," he responds warmly, his expression conveying empathy and understanding. "Strength-based leadership fosters a positive organizational culture by creating an environment where individuals feel valued, empowered, and appreciated for their unique strengths. By focusing on strengths rather than weaknesses, leaders can cultivate a culture of collaboration, innovation, and resilience."

Lastly, Director Patel, known for his attention to detail, offers his question. "What steps can leaders take to develop their own strength-based leadership skills?" he inquires, his voice measured and deliberate.

James nods approvingly at Patel's question, recognizing its practical significance. "An insightful inquiry, Patel," he replies, his tone conveying a sense of encouragement and guidance. "Leaders can develop their strength-based leadership skills through self-awareness, continuous learning, and practice. This may involve conducting strengths assessments, seeking feedback from peers and mentors, and actively seeking opportunities to apply strength-based approaches in their leadership roles."

With each question addressed, the room brims with renewed insight and understanding. James' articulate responses have not only illuminated the essence of strength-based leadership but have also ignited a collective drive among the directors to embrace and embody these principles in their own leadership journey.

As the morning session draws to a close, James gestures towards the clock with a smile. "It's time for a well-deserved break," he announces, his voice ringing with warmth and enthusiasm. "Let's reconvene after lunch to continue our discussions."

With a collective sigh of relief, the team rises from their seats, eager to stretch their legs and refuel for the rest of the day. Conversations buzz with excitement as they file out of the boardroom, the anticipation of what's to come lingering in the air.

Outside the confines of the meeting room, the team disperses, each member heading in search of sustenance and respite. Some opt for a leisurely stroll around the office grounds, while others gravitate towards the nearby cafeteria, drawn by the promise of a hearty meal.

Amidst the chatter and laughter, James pauses for a moment, taking in the sight before him with a sense of satisfaction. It's moments like these, he thinks to himself, that foster friendship and strengthen bonds within the team.

As the lunch break comes to an end, the team begins to trickle back into the boardroom, their spirits rejuvenated and their minds ready for the afternoon ahead. With a renewed sense of purpose, they settle back into their seats, eager to pick up where they left off and continue their journey towards organizational excellence.

As the clock strikes 3:00 PM, signaling the end of their lunch break, the team filters back into the boardroom, refreshed and ready to resume their discussions. James stands at the front of the room, a sense of purpose emanating from his every movement. With a click of his remote, the PowerPoint presentation springs to life on the screen behind him, illuminating the outline for the afternoon's session.

"Welcome back, everyone," James greets them warmly, his voice carrying across the room with authority. "I hope you all had a chance to recharge during the break."

The team settles into their seats, anticipation building as James prepares to delve into the topic of developing a strength mindset. With a confident click, he advances to the first slide of the presentation.

"Let's jump right in," James begins, his voice steady and assured. "We're going to explore the concept of a strength mindset and its importance in driving success within our organization."

As James speaks, the room is bathed in the soft glow of the projector, the words on the screen serving as a roadmap for their discussion.

"First, let's define what we mean by a strength mindset," James continues, his eyes scanning the room to ensure he has everyone's attention. "Then, we'll discuss why it's so crucial for

CHAPTER FOUR: THE FOUNDATION OF STRENGTH-BASED LEADERSHIP

each of us to cultivate this mindset in our professional lives."

The team listens intently as James elaborates on each point of the outline, his words accompanied by engaging visuals and real-life examples. With each slide, the depth of his knowledge and passion for the topic becomes increasingly evident.

"Understanding our strengths is the first step towards developing a strength mindset," James explains, his voice resonating with conviction. "We'll explore how to identify our own strengths and recognize the unique talents of those around us."

As the presentation progresses, James seamlessly transitions from one topic to the next, guiding the team through a comprehensive exploration of the subject matter.

"Cultivating a strength mindset isn't just about acknowledging our strengths," James emphasizes, his words echoing through the room. "It's about embracing growth, overcoming challenges, and fostering resilience in the face of adversity."

The team nods in agreement, fully captivated by James' insights and inspired by his passion for the topic. With each passing minute, they feel more empowered to embrace a strength mindset and apply it to their work and personal lives.

"As we wrap up today's session," James concludes, his voice tinged with optimism, "let's remember the importance of continuing to develop our strength mindset. Together, we can create a future filled with growth, success, and endless possibilities."

As James wraps up his compelling discussion on "Developing a Strengths Mindset," the directors, eager to delve deeper into the topic, prepare to pose their questions, their faces reflecting a mix of anticipation and intellectual curiosity.

Director Smith, known for his probing inquiries, is the first to raise his hand. "How can individuals overcome self-limiting beliefs to embrace a strengths mindset?" he asks, his tone reflecting a blend of skepticism and genuine interest.

James nods thoughtfully, acknowledging the significance of Smith's question. "A pertinent question, Smith," he responds, his voice resonating with empathy and understanding. "Overcoming self-limiting beliefs requires introspection and self-awareness. By reframing negative thoughts and focusing on their strengths, individuals can gradually shift their mindset towards one of empowerment and possibility."

Director Rodriguez, renowned for her strategic insights, follows up with her question. "What role does leadership play in fostering a strengths mindset within an organization?" she inquires, her expression conveying a thirst for knowledge.

James smiles, recognizing the relevance of Rodriguez's query. "An excellent point, Rodriguez," he replies warmly, his demeanor poised and engaging. "Leadership plays a crucial role in fostering a strengths mindset by setting the tone from the top, providing support and encouragement, and modeling strength-based behaviors in their interactions with employees."

Director Chen, with her emphasis on employee well-being, poses her question next. "How can organizations create a culture that encourages the development of a strengths mindset among employees?" she asks, her voice tinged with genuine concern.

James nods empathetically, acknowledging the importance of Chen's inquiry. "A thoughtful question, Chen," he responds warmly, his expression conveying empathy and understanding. "Organizations can create a culture that encourages the development of a strengths mindset by offering training and development programs, promoting open communication and feedback, and recognizing and celebrating individual strengths."

Lastly, Director Patel, known for his attention to detail, offers his question. "What practical steps can individuals take to cultivate a strengths mindset in their daily lives?" he inquires, his voice measured and deliberate.

James nods approvingly at Patel's question, recognizing its practical significance. "An insightful inquiry, Patel," he replies, his tone conveying a sense of encouragement and guidance. "Individuals can cultivate a strengths mindset by practicing gratitude, setting goals aligned with their strengths, and surrounding themselves with supportive networks that encourage growth and development."

With each question addressed, the room brims with renewed insight and understanding. James' articulate responses have not only illuminated the path to developing a strengths mindset but have also inspired the directors to embark on their own journey of self-discovery and growth.

With a final click of his remote, James dims the projector, the room bathed in a soft glow as the screen fades to black. The team applauds, their hearts full of gratitude for the valuable insights they've gained and the journey they've embarked upon together. As they prepare to adjourn for the day, they do so with a renewed sense of purpose and a shared vision for the future.

As the presentation concludes and the room erupts into applause, the CEO rises from his seat, a proud smile playing on his lips. He moves to stand beside James, extending a hand in gratitude.

"James, that was an exceptional presentation," the CEO commends, his voice filled with genuine appreciation. "You've done a fantastic job of guiding us through this important topic."

James accepts the CEO's handshake with a humble nod, his expression a mix of pride and humility. "Thank you, sir," he responds, his voice steady despite the swell of emotions within him. "It was an honor to lead the discussion."

The CEO's gaze sweeps over the room, meeting the eyes of each team member in turn. "As we move forward," he continues, his tone carrying the weight of authority, "I'll be taking the reins for our next presentation."

A ripple of anticipation courses through the room at the CEO's announcement, the team leaning forward in their seats to catch every word.

"With your support and guidance, I'm confident that we'll continue to drive our organization forward," the CEO asserts, his voice resonating with unwavering determination.

As the meeting draws to a close, the team members exchange knowing glances, their minds already racing with ideas for the CEO's upcoming presentation. With James' stellar example fresh in their minds, they feel inspired and empowered to rise to the challenge ahead.

With a final word of thanks and a promise to reconvene soon, the CEO bids the team farewell, his heart filled with pride for their accomplishments and anticipation for the journey that lies ahead. As they disperse from the boardroom, the air crackles with excitement, each team member eager to play their part in shaping the future of the organization.

5

Chapter Five: Identifying and Assessing Strengths

As the first light of Monday morning filters through the windows of the boardroom, casting a soft glow over the sleek conference table, the team members begin to filter in one by one, their footsteps echoing in the hushed silence. Anticipation hangs heavy in the air, each member eager to reconvene after the weekend hiatus.

At exactly 9:00 AM, the CEO strides into the room, his presence commanding attention as he takes his place at the head of the table. With a confident nod to his assembled team, he clears his throat, preparing to address them.

"Good morning, everyone," the CEO begins, his voice cutting through the stillness like a knife. "I trust you all had a restful weekend and are ready to dive back into our work with renewed vigor."

The team responds with a chorus of murmured greetings and nods of agreement, their eyes fixed on the CEO with rapt attention.

"As we gather here today," the CEO continues, his tone

measured and authoritative, "I'm excited to announce that we'll be delving into a new topic: identifying and assessing strengths."

A ripple of interest sweeps through the room at the CEO's words, each team member leaning forward in their seats in anticipation of what's to come.

As the team gathers once more in the boardroom, the CEO stands at the front, ready to guide them through the intricacies of strength assessment. With a click of the remote, the PowerPoint presentation illuminates the screen, casting a glow of anticipation over the room.

He gestures toward the first slide, where the words "Introduction" are displayed in bold letters. "At the heart of our discussion lies the importance of strength assessment," he continues, his words carrying the weight of conviction. "By understanding and harnessing our individual strengths, we unlock the potential for personal and professional growth."

As the slides transition, the CEO delves into the various tools and techniques available for strength assessment. "From self-assessment to feedback mechanisms," he explains, "each method offers unique insights into our strengths and areas for development."

With each point he makes, the CEO pauses to allow the information to sink in, his eyes scanning the room for signs of engagement. "Let's begin with self-assessment," he says, his voice steady and sure. "By understanding our personal strengths through reflection exercises and self-discovery questionnaires, we lay the foundation for growth and self-awareness."

As the presentation progresses, the CEO explores the importance of feedback mechanisms in the assessment process. "360-degree feedback, peer reviews, and performance appraisals," he explains, "offer valuable insights from multiple perspectives, helping us gain a holistic understanding of our strengths and areas for improvement."

Next, the CEO turns his attention to strengths-based interviews, highlighting the role of structured questions and real-world case studies in uncovering hidden talents. "Through structured interviews and behavioral assessments," he says, "we can identify the unique strengths that drive individual and team success."

As the presentation nears its conclusion, the CEO explores the role of psychometric assessments, observation and evaluation, and coaching and mentoring in the assessment process. "By integrating data and analysis," he concludes, "we gain valuable insights into our strengths, enabling us to chart a course toward future success."

With a final click of the remote, the CEO brings the presentation to a close, leaving the team with a sense of clarity and purpose. "Let us embrace the power of strength assessment," he says, his voice filled with conviction. "Together, we can unlock the full potential of our organization and pave the way for a future of growth and success."

The clock strikes noon, and a gentle chime fills the air, signaling the much-awaited lunch break. The CEO, his voice steady and commanding, announces, "It's time for a well-deserved break, everyone. Let's reconvene here in one hour."

With a collective sigh of relief, the team members rise from their seats, their faces alight with anticipation for the respite that awaits them. They exchange friendly nods and smiles, a sense of friendship binding them together as they make their way out of the boardroom.

As they step into the hallway, the atmosphere is alive with

the buzz of conversation and laughter, a welcome respite from the intensity of the morning's discussions. Some head to the cafeteria, eager to indulge in a hearty meal and catch up with colleagues, while others opt for a leisurely stroll outside, basking in the warmth of the midday sun.

Amidst the hustle and bustle, the CEO stands at the center of it all, a beacon of calm and composure amidst the chaos. He watches with a sense of satisfaction as his team members disperse, knowing that they will return refreshed and rejuvenated, ready to tackle the challenges that lie ahead.

As the minutes tick by, the boardroom gradually empties, until only the CEO remains, his thoughts consumed by the tasks that await him in the afternoon session. With a final glance at his watch, he nods to himself in satisfaction, knowing that the lunch break has served its purpose in reenergizing both body and mind.

With renewed determination, the CEO takes a deep breath and heads off in search of sustenance, his mind already racing ahead to the discussions that await him in the afternoon. For now, though, it is time to savor the simple pleasures of food, friendship, and a well-deserved break.

As the clock strikes 1:00 PM, the team filters back into the boardroom, their anticipation deep in the air. The CEO stands at the head of the table, his eyes alight with enthusiasm as he prepares to guide them through the intricacies of strength-based interviews and feedbacks.

"Welcome back, everyone," he begins, his voice projecting confidence and warmth as he gestures toward the PowerPoint presentation displayed on the screen behind him. "This afternoon, we embark on a journey to explore the importance and power of strength-based interviews and feedbacks."

With a click of the remote, the CEO advances to the first slide, the vibrant colors illuminating the room with a sense of purpose. "Let us begin with the foundation," he says, his words carrying the weight of authority. "The importance of strength-based interviews and feedbacks cannot be overstated. They are the cornerstone of organizational development, guiding us toward a future of growth and success."

As the CEO speaks, the slides transition seamlessly, each one unveiling a new facet of the topic at hand. "We'll start by delving into the essence of strength-based interviews," he continues, his voice steady and sure. "Defined by their focus on individual strengths, these interviews are designed to uncover hidden talents and unleash untapped potential."

With each point he makes, the CEO pauses to allow the information to sink in, his eyes scanning the room for signs of comprehension and engagement. "Next, we'll explore the art of conducting strength-based interviews," he explains, his words punctuated by nods of agreement from the team. "From preparing thoughtful questions to creating a welcoming atmosphere, every detail plays a crucial role in eliciting meaningful responses."

As the presentation progresses, the CEO delves deeper into the nuances of providing strength-based feedback, highlighting the importance of constructive criticism and supportive guidance. "Feedback is a gift," he emphasizes, his voice tinged with sincerity. "When delivered with care and intention, it has the power to inspire growth and foster a culture of continuous improvement."

With each passing slide, the CEO paints a vivid picture of the transformative impact of strength-based approaches on performance management and team dynamics. "Through real-world examples and case studies," he concludes, his tone filled with conviction, "we'll witness the profound effect that these strategies can have on organizational outcomes."

As the CEO wraps up his detailed explanations on "Tools and Techniques for Strengths Assessment" and "Strengths-Based Interviews and Feedback," he opens the floor to questions, inviting the directors to share their thoughts and seek clarification.

Director Smith, known for his analytical mind, raises his hand first. "Could you elaborate on how we can ensure the validity and reliability of the assessment tools we use?" he inquires, his tone measured and precise.

The CEO nods appreciatively, recognizing the importance of addressing concerns about the credibility of assessment methods. "Certainly, Smith," he responds, his voice steady and confident. "Ensuring the validity and reliability of assessment tools requires rigorous validation processes, including pilot testing, psychometric analysis, and ongoing refinement based on empirical evidence."

Next, Director Johnson, known for her insightful queries, seeks clarification. "How can we tailor strengths-based interviews to different roles and levels within the organization?" she asks, her curiosity evident in her thoughtful expression.

The CEO acknowledges the relevance of Director Johnson's question, his gaze thoughtful as he formulates his response. "Customizing strengths-based interviews involves aligning questions with the specific competencies and requirements of each role," he explains, his words resonating with practical wisdom. "By tailoring our approach, we can ensure that the interview process effectively captures the unique strengths and potential of each candidate."

Lastly, Director Garcia, renowned for her strategic perspective, raises a question regarding feedback mechanisms. "How can we foster a culture of constructive feedback to support ongoing growth and development?" she queries, her voice imbued with a sense of forward-thinking vision.

The CEO nods approvingly at Director Garcia's question, recognizing its significance in nurturing a culture of continuous improvement. "Building a culture of constructive feedback begins with fostering psychological safety and trust," he asserts, his demeanor authoritative yet empathetic. "Encouraging open communication, providing timely and specific feedback, and promoting a growth mindset are essential components of this process."

With the directors' questions addressed comprehensively, the CEO draws the discussion to a close, his concluding remarks infused with a sense of purpose and determination. "As we move forward, let us remain committed to leveraging these tools and techniques to unlock the full potential of our teams," he asserts, his words resonating with conviction. "Together, we can cultivate a culture of strengths and excellence that propels us towards our collective goals."

With a sense of clarity and purpose, the team concludes the session, empowered by their newfound insights and ready to embark on the journey of harnessing strengths for organizational success.

As the presentation draws to a close, the CEO leaves the team with a final message of encouragement. "Let us embrace the power of strength-based interviews and feedbacks," he says, his voice ringing with passion. "Together, we can unlock the full potential of our organization and chart a course toward a future filled with growth, success, and endless possibilities."

As the CEO finishes his presentation, he looks around the

room, observing the attentive expressions of his team members. With a nod of satisfaction, he announces, "Let's take a short break for tea and refreshments."

The tension in the room eases as the team members rise from their seats, stretching their limbs after the intense session. Conversations buzz softly as they make their way to the refreshment area, eager for a moment of relaxation.

In the break room, the atmosphere is lively yet relaxed. Colleagues exchange pleasantries and share anecdotes from the morning's discussion. The aroma of freshly brewed tea fills the air, mingling with the scent of pastries and snacks laid out on the table.

The CEO joins in the conversations, mingling with his team members as they enjoy their refreshments. Despite the brief respite, the energy in the room remains intense, fueled by the anticipation of the discussions to come.

As the break draws to a close, the CEO glances at his watch and nods to the team. "Shall we reconvene in fifteen minutes?" he suggests, his voice carrying across the room. With reluctant smiles, the team members begin to make their way back to the boardroom, recharged and ready to tackle the rest of the day's agenda.

As the clock strikes 4:00 PM, the team gathers once more, anticipation buzzing in the air as they await the CEO's guidance on the pivotal topic ahead. With a commanding presence, the CEO takes the floor, his eyes alight with purpose.

"Good afternoon, everyone," he begins, his voice resonating with authority and conviction. "Today, we embark on a journey to explore the creation of a strengths inventory for our organization."

In the introductory segment, the CEO wastes no time in

emphasizing the critical importance of understanding and leveraging strengths within the organization. "Our ability to harness the unique talents and capabilities of our team members is paramount to our success," he declares. "Let us delve into the process of creating a strengths inventory to unlock our full potential."

With a clear sense of direction, the CEO proceeds to outline the steps involved in creating a strengths inventory, starting with *assessing organizational needs and goals.* "Before we embark on this journey, we must first understand why we are doing it and what we hope to achieve," he explains. "Our strengths inventory must align closely with our organizational objectives and vision."

Moving forward, the CEO emphasizes the importance of *identifying key stakeholders* who will be involved in the process. "Creating a strengths inventory is a collaborative effort," he asserts. "We must engage leadership and relevant departments to ensure buy-in and alignment."

With meticulous attention to detail, the CEO guides the team through *defining strengths criteria and selecting assessment tools* that align with the organization's goals and culture. "We must establish clear criteria for evaluating strengths and choose assessment tools that will provide meaningful insights," he advises.

As the discussion unfolds, the CEO leads the team through the process of *conducting assessments, analyzing data, and creating the strengths inventory.* "Through careful analysis of assessment results, we can identify patterns and trends in our strengths," he states. "This will allow us to compile a comprehensive inventory that captures the essence of our organization's capabilities."

With unwavering focus, the CEO underscores the importance of *utilizing the strengths inventory* to inform talent management processes and decision-making. "Our strengths inventory will serve as a valuable resource for identifying opportunities, allocating resources, and maximizing our organizational effectiveness," he affirms.

In the final segments, the CEO emphasizes the importance of *regularly reviewing and updating the strengths inventory* to ensure its relevance and accuracy over time. "Creating a strengths inventory is not a one-time effort," he concludes. "It requires ongoing attention and commitment to ensure its effectiveness in driving organizational success."

With a resounding call to action, the CEO concludes the discussion, leaving the team inspired and empowered to embark on the journey of creating a strengths inventory for their organization. "Together, let us harness the power of our collective strengths to propel us towards a future of unprecedented success," he declares, his words echoing in the minds of all who are present.

With a nod of finality, the CEO brings the meeting to a close, his demeanor a blend of satisfaction and purpose. "Thank you, everyone," he says, his voice carrying the weight of authority tempered with warmth. "Let's continue to build upon the momentum we've created here today."

As if on cue, the team members rise from their seats, a sense of purpose infusing their movements as they prepare to depart. Conversations buzz with renewed energy, the air crackling with anticipation for the tasks ahead.

With a last glance around the boardroom, the CEO offers a reassuring smile, his confidence a beacon of reassurance for the team. "Until next time," he says, his words a promise of future collaboration and success.

As the door closes behind them, the echoes of the meeting linger in the air, a testament to the shared commitment and dedication of all who were present. And with that, they disperse, each carrying with them the seeds of inspiration planted during their time together.

6

Chapter Six: Building a Strength-Based Culture

The clock strikes 9:00 AM on a Tuesday, signaling the commencement of a pivotal gathering in the heart of the organization. As the CEO enters the boardroom, a wave of anticipation rippled through the assembled participants. With a congenial smile, he extends a warm welcome, his presence infusing the atmosphere with a sense of purpose and direction.

"Good morning, everyone," the CEO's voice resonates with authority as he addresses the attentive audience. "Today marks the beginning of a crucial discussion on fostering a positive organizational climate. Without further ado, I'll hand over the reins to James, our esteemed director of human resources, to guide us through this enlightening session."

With a gracious nod, the CEO passes the torch to James, who steps forward with a confident stride. His demeanor exudes a blend of professionalism and approachability, instantly commanding the room's attention.

"Thank you, CEO," James begins, his voice imbued with

CHAPTER SIX: BUILDING A STRENGTH-BASED CULTURE

a sense of passion for the topic at hand. "Good morning, everyone. It's truly a pleasure to be here today to delve into the critical subject of fostering a positive organizational climate."

As James speaks, he projects an air of authority, backed by a deep well of knowledge and expertise. With a subtle click, the room was bathed in the soft glow of the projector, illuminating the screen behind him with a vibrant display of colors and graphics.

"Let's dive right in," James continues, his tone brimming with enthusiasm. "Fostering a positive organizational climate is not just a goal—it's a journey, one that requires dedication, collaboration, and a shared commitment to excellence."

With each slide, James paints a vivid picture of the elements that contributed to a positive climate within an organization. From trust and communication to collaboration and employee engagement, he dissects each component with precision, offering insights gleaned from years of experience and research.

As the presentation unfolds, the participants lean in, hanging on James's every word. His passion for the subject was contagious, igniting a spark of inspiration in each member of the audience.

And so, against the backdrop of the illuminated screen and the attentive gaze of the assembled team, James embarks on a journey of exploration and enlightenment, guiding them towards a future filled with positivity, productivity, and unparalleled success.

"Leadership," James continues, his tone infused with a blend of reverence and determination, "serves as the bedrock upon which this culture is built. It's not merely about holding a title or occupying a corner office—it's about inspiring, guiding, and empowering those around you to reach their fullest potential."

With each successive slide, James delves deeper into the strategies and tactics that leaders could employ to cultivate a supportive and inclusive environment. He speaks of the importance of leading by example, of fostering open communication and trust, and of creating opportunities for meaningful growth and development.

"As leaders," James emphasizes, his words ringing with conviction, "it's our responsibility to create a safe space where individuals feel encouraged to step into their strengths, to take risks, and to pursue excellence without fear of judgment or reprisal."

As the discussion on "Fostering a Positive Organizational Climate" reaches its peak, the directors, eager to delve deeper into the topic, raise thought-provoking questions, prompting James, the facilitator, to provide further insights.

Director Smith, known for his attention to detail, raises his hand first. "How can we measure the effectiveness of our efforts in fostering a positive organizational climate?" he asks, his tone reflective of his analytical mindset.

James nods thoughtfully at Director Smith's question, acknowledging its significance in assessing the impact of organizational initiatives. "Measuring the effectiveness of our efforts requires a combination of quantitative and qualitative indicators," he explains, his words infused with clarity and assurance. "Key metrics such as employee satisfaction surveys, turnover rates, and productivity levels can provide valuable insights into the overall health of our organizational climate."

Director Johnson, renowned for her empathetic approach, seeks clarification. "What role do leadership behaviors play in shaping the organizational climate?" she inquires, her tone empathetic yet probing.

CHAPTER SIX: BUILDING A STRENGTH-BASED CULTURE

James appreciates Director Johnson's question, recognizing the pivotal role of leadership in setting the tone for organizational culture. "Leadership behaviors serve as a cornerstone of organizational climate," he responds, his voice resonating with conviction. "By demonstrating authenticity, transparency, and empathy, leaders can inspire trust, foster collaboration, and cultivate a sense of belonging among employees."

Lastly, Director Garcia, known for her strategic vision, raises a question regarding sustainability. "How can we ensure that our efforts to foster a positive organizational climate are sustainable in the long term?" she asks, her tone reflecting her forward-thinking mindset.

James nods in agreement with Director Garcia's inquiry, acknowledging the importance of sustainability in organizational initiatives. "Sustainability hinges on embedding positive practices into our organizational culture and aligning them with our core values," he explains, his words infused with wisdom and foresight. "By continuously reinforcing positive behaviors, fostering a culture of accountability, and adapting to changing dynamics, we can ensure that our efforts endure over time."

With the directors' questions addressed comprehensively, James draws the discussion to a close, his concluding remarks imbued with a sense of optimism and purpose. "As we strive to cultivate a positive organizational climate, let us remain committed to fostering a culture of respect, collaboration, and continuous improvement," he asserts, his words resonating with clarity and determination. "Together, we can create an environment where every individual feels valued, empowered, and inspired to contribute their best."

With a renewed sense of purpose and direction, the team

concludes the session, empowered by their collective insights and ready to embark on the journey of fostering a positive organizational climate for sustained success.

As the applause gradually subsides, the CEO rises from his seat, a warm smile gracing his features. "Thank you, James, for that enlightening discourse," he says, his voice resonating with genuine appreciation. "Now, let's break for lunch."

With those words, the tension in the room seem to dissipate, replaced by an air of anticipation for the upcoming meal. Conversations buzz among the attendees as they gather their belongings and make their way toward the door, their appetites whet not just for food, but for the possibilities that lay ahead.

Outside the boardroom, the aroma of freshly prepared dishes greet them, beckoning them toward the communal dining area. Plates clink, laughter ring out, and friendships are forged over shared meals—a fitting interlude in the midst of a day filled with inspiration and enlightenment.

As the clock struck 1:00 PM, the team filters back into the boardroom, their expressions a mixture of anticipation and eagerness. James, the Director of Human Resources, stands at the front of the room, ready to resume the day's proceedings. With a confident yet welcoming smile, he beckons the attendees to settle back into their seats, signaling the beginning of the second session.

"Welcome back, everyone," James begins, his voice projecting authority and warmth in equal measure. "In this session, we'll delve into the crucial topic of communicating the value of strengths to our employees."

A hush fell over the room as James launches into his presentation, the slides on the projector screen behind him serving as a visual aid to his words. Each slide illuminate the importance of fostering a culture that not only recognizes but celebrates the unique strengths of every individual within the organization.

With eloquence and conviction, James articulate strategies for effectively conveying this message to employees at all levels. He emphasizes the power of storytelling, encouraging managers to share personal anecdotes that highlight the transformative impact of leveraging strengths in the workplace.

"As leaders, it's imperative that we not only recognize the value of strengths but also communicate this value effectively to our teams," James proclaims, his voice resounding with conviction. "By doing so, we empower our employees to embrace their strengths fully, paving the way for enhanced collaboration, innovation, and overall success."

With pens poised and minds primed, the team embark on a journey of collective ideation. James, their guide in this creative endeavor, stands at the forefront, encouraging everyone to unleash their imagination.

"Let's dive into the heart of it," James declares, his voice brimming with energy. "How can we seamlessly integrate strengths-based principles into our everyday practices?"

As ideas begin to flow like a river, James meticulously captures each suggestion on the whiteboard, ensuring that no valuable insight goes unnoticed. From reimagining performance evaluations to revamping feedback mechanisms, the possibilities seemed endless.

"We need to ensure that these initiatives resonate with our organizational values," James emphasizes, his tone unwavering. "Consistency is key if we're to cultivate a culture that truly embraces strengths."

With each idea that emerges, the room buzz with excitement, a deep sense of enthusiasm infusing the atmosphere. Collaboratively, they explore innovative approaches to recognizing and celebrating individual strengths, envisioning a workplace where every voice is heard and every contribution valued.

As the discussion on "Communicating the Values of Strengths to Employees" unfolds, the directors eagerly raise questions, prompting James, the facilitator, to provide further clarity and guidance.

Director Smith, known for his meticulous attention to detail, raises his hand first. "How can we effectively communicate the values of strengths to employees across different levels of the organization?" he asks, his tone reflective of his analytical mindset.

James nods appreciatively at Director Smith's question, recognizing the importance of tailored communication strategies. "Effectively communicating the values of strengths requires a multi-faceted approach," he responds, his voice resonating with authority. "It involves utilizing various channels such as town hall meetings, team workshops, and digital platforms to ensure that our message reaches employees at all levels."

Director Johnson, renowned for her empathetic approach, seeks clarification. "How can we address potential resistance or skepticism among employees towards embracing strengths-based approaches?" she inquires, her tone empathetic yet probing.

James acknowledges Director Johnson's question, understanding the significance of addressing resistance with empathy and understanding. "Addressing resistance requires transparency, empathy, and open dialogue," he explains, his words infused with empathy. "By actively listening to employees' concerns, providing reassurance, and highlighting the benefits of strengths-based approaches, we can foster a culture of

CHAPTER SIX: BUILDING A STRENGTH-BASED CULTURE

acceptance and engagement."

Lastly, Director Garcia, known for her strategic vision, raises a question regarding alignment. "How can we ensure that our communication efforts align with the organizational values and goals?" she asks, her tone reflecting her strategic mindset.

James nods in agreement with Director Garcia's inquiry, recognizing the importance of alignment in communication strategies. "Ensuring alignment requires a clear understanding of our organizational values and goals," he responds, his words infused with clarity and purpose. "By anchoring our communication efforts in our core values and linking them to our strategic objectives, we can create a compelling narrative that resonates with employees and inspires action."

With the directors' questions addressed comprehensively, James draws the discussion to a close, his concluding remarks imbued with a sense of conviction and purpose. "As we strive to communicate the values of strengths to employees, let us remain committed to fostering a culture of empowerment, growth, and collaboration," he asserts, his words resonating with clarity and determination. "Together, we can empower our employees to unleash their full potential and drive organizational success."

With a renewed sense of clarity and purpose, the team concludes the session, empowered by their collective insights and ready to embark on the journey of communicating the values of strengths to employees with purpose and conviction.

As the brainstorming session draws to a close, James surveys the array of ideas before him, a sense of pride evident in his gaze. "I'm incredibly impressed by the creativity and dedication displayed here today," he remarks, his words a testament to the collective spirit of the team.

With a renewed sense of purpose, they resolve to transform these ideas into actionable strategies, poised to embark on a journey of transformation that will redefine the very fabric of their organization.

As James concludes his presentation, the room erupts into a chorus of applause, a tangible expression of appreciation for the insights he has shared. With a nod of gratitude to his attentive audience, James steps back, ready to field any questions or engage in further discussion on this vital topic.

As James conclude his insightful remarks, a sense of accomplishment settles over the room like a warm blanket. With a gracious smile, he nods to the team, signalling the end of the second session.

"Let's take a well-deserved break," he announces, his voice laced with a touch of cheerfulness. "I believe a cup of tea is in order to rejuvenate our spirits."

With that, the team members begin to stretch their limbs, exchanging nods of appreciation and smiles of satisfaction. Conversations buzz softly in the air as they make their way to the refreshment area, eager to recharge both body and mind.

Amidst the clinking of cups and the aroma of freshly brewed tea, camaraderie blossom effortlessly. Laughter echoed across the room, weaving a tapestry of shared moments and cherished memories.

As they sip their tea and nibble on light snacks, the team finds solace in the simple act of coming together. Bonds are strengthened, friendships deepen, and a sense of unity flourishes amidst the tranquil pause.

With each passing moment, the tea break serve as a gentle reminder of the importance of taking time to rest and reconnect. Energized and revitalized, they are ready to embark on the next leg of their journey, fueled by the warmth of camaraderie and the promise of new beginnings.

As the clock strikes 4:00 PM, the team reconvenes, their energy palpable as they prepared for the final session of the day. James, with a sense of purpose in his stride, step forward to lead the discussion on aligning organizational values with individual strengths.

"Welcome back, everyone," James greets with a warm smile, his voice carrying a sense of anticipation for what lay ahead. "Let's dive into our last session for today."

With a subtle click, the projector hum to life, casting a soft glow across the room as James begins to elucidate on the intricacies of aligning organizational values with individual strengths. His words carry weight, each syllable infused with wisdom and insight garnered from years of experience.

"As we navigate the complex landscape of organizational dynamics," James begins, his tone measured yet resolute, "it becomes imperative to forge a symbiotic relationship between our core values and the unique strengths of each individual."

With a deft touch, he outlines strategies for fostering a culture where organizational values serve as guiding beacons, illuminating the path towards personal and collective growth. Through poignant anecdotes and real-world examples, he paints a vivid picture of the transformative power of alignment.

"As we harness the collective brilliance of our team," James continues, his passion igniting a spark within each listener, "we pave the way for innovation, collaboration, and unparalleled success."

As his words linger in the air, a sense of unity envelope the room, binding them together in a shared vision of greatness. With each passing moment, they draw closer to the realization that true strength lies not only in individual prowess but in the harmonious synergy of values and strengths.

As the discussion unfold, James and the directors gather around the table, their minds buzzing with anticipation for the task at hand. With charts and graphs strewn across the surface, they delve deep into the intricacies of developing a communication plan for cascading strength-based messages throughout the organization.

"Communication is key," James emphasize, his voice carrying the weight of conviction. "We must ensure that every member of our organization is not only aware of our strength-based approach but fully embraces it."

Nods of agreement ripple through the room as the directors lean in, eager to contribute their insights to the conversation. Together, they brainstorm tactics for engaging employees at all levels, recognizing the importance of building momentum for cultural transformation from the ground up.

"We need to create a ripple effect," one director suggests, her eyes alight with enthusiasm. "By empowering our frontline employees to champion our strength-based initiatives, we can inspire a sense of ownership and accountability throughout the organization."

James nod in approval, his mind already spinning with ideas for harnessing the collective power of their workforce. "Let's leverage our internal communication channels," he proposes, his voice brimming with confidence. "From town hall meetings to newsletters, we have a plethora of platforms at our disposal to amplify our message."

As they huddle together, their pens dancing across the page, a sense of friendship envelope the room. With each idea shared and refined, they draw closer to crafting a communication plan that will ignite a spark of inspiration in every corner of the organization.

Hours pass in a blur as they meticulously map out their strategy, leaving no stone unturned in their quest to foster a culture of strength and resilience. And as the final details fell into place, they emerge from the meeting room with a renewed sense of purpose, ready to embark on the journey of cultural transformation armed with a communication plan that would set their organization ablaze with possibility.

As James wraps up his comprehensive discussion on aligning organizational values with individual strengths, the room is filled with a sense of anticipation as the directors prepare to pose their questions.

Director Smith, known for his meticulous attention to detail, raises his hand first. "How do we ensure that our organizational values remain relevant and adaptable in the face of changing workforce dynamics?" he asks, his voice carrying a note of concern tinged with curiosity.

James acknowledges Director Smith's question with a nod, recognizing the importance of adaptability in maintaining alignment. "Adapting our organizational values requires ongoing reflection and a willingness to embrace change," he responds, his tone reflecting a sense of assurance and clarity. "By soliciting feedback from employees and stakeholders and remaining open to new perspectives, we can ensure that our values evolve in step with our workforce."

Director Johnson, known for her empathetic leadership style, poses a question centered on inclusivity. "How can we ensure that all employees feel valued and respected, regardless of their strengths or backgrounds?" she inquires, her tone conveying a genuine concern for fostering a supportive workplace culture.

James listens attentively to Director Johnson's question, recognizing its importance in promoting a culture of belonging and acceptance. "Creating an inclusive environment begins with embracing the diversity of strengths and perspectives within our workforce," he explains, his words infused with empathy and understanding. "By celebrating the unique contributions of each individual and fostering a culture of respect and appreciation, we can ensure that all employees feel valued and empowered to succeed."

Director Garcia, known for her strategic insight, seeks clarification on implementation strategies. "What specific steps can we take to embed our organizational values into daily operations and decision-making processes?" she asks, her tone reflecting a desire for practical guidance.

James acknowledges Director Garcia's question, recognizing the significance of operationalizing values in driving organizational alignment. "Integrating our values into daily operations requires a multi-faceted approach," he responds, his words resonating with clarity and purpose. "By aligning performance metrics, decision-making frameworks, and leadership practices with our values, we can ensure that they guide our actions and behaviors at every level of the organization."

Lastly, Director Martinez, known for her innovative thinking, raises a question about adaptability. "How can we encourage a culture of continuous learning and growth to support the ongoing alignment of organizational values with individual strengths?" she inquires, her tone reflecting a forward-thinking approach.

James considers Director Martinez's question thoughtfully, recognizing the importance of fostering a culture of agility and innovation. "Encouraging a culture of continuous learning begins with leadership commitment and organizational support," he explains, his words infused with optimism and possibility. "By providing opportunities for skill development, feedback, and recognition, we can empower employees to embrace change and adapt their strengths to meet evolving organizational needs."

With the directors' questions addressed comprehensively, James prepares to offer his concluding remarks on the topic. "As we strive to align organizational values with individual strengths, let us remain committed to fostering a culture of authenticity, collaboration, and growth," he asserts, his voice resonating with conviction and purpose. "Together, we can harness the power of our collective strengths to drive organizational success and create a workplace where every individual thrives."

With a renewed sense of clarity and purpose, the team concludes the session, empowered by their collective insights and ready to embark on the journey of aligning organizational values with individual strengths with determination and resolve.

With a final flourish, James concludes the session, leaving the team inspired and invigorated, ready to embark on the journey of aligning organizational values with individual strengths. As they file out of the room, a sense of purpose infuse their every step, propelling them towards a future illuminated by the promise of endless possibilities.

As the discussions draws to a close, the CEO rises from his seat, his presence commanding the attention of everyone in the room. With a warm smile, he begins his final remarks, his words infused with wisdom and gravitas.

"My dear colleagues," he begins, his voice resonating with

sincerity, "today has been a day of profound insight and collaboration. Together, we have explored the depths of strength-based leadership, laying the groundwork for a future of growth and success."

His words hung in the air, eliciting nods of agreement and murmurs of approval from the assembled team. With each passing moment, the CEO's passion for their shared vision becomes profound, infusing the room with a sense of purpose and determination.

"As we move forward," he continues, his gaze sweeping across the room, "let us carry with us the lessons we have learned today. Let us embrace the power of strengths, both individually and collectively, as we strive to build a culture of excellence and innovation."

The room fell silent, the weight of the CEO's words settling upon them like a comforting mantle. In that moment, they feel united in their purpose, bound together by a shared commitment to realize their organization's full potential.

With a final nod of encouragement, the CEO concludes his remarks, his words lingering in the air long after he has returned to his seat. And as the team disperses, their hearts filled with renewed determination, they know that the journey ahead will be challenging, but with the CEO's guidance and their collective strength, they are ready to face whatever lay ahead.

7

Chapter seven: Leveraging Strengths for Team Performance

At exactly 9:00 AM on a Wednesday morning, the CEO stands at the head of the boardroom table, commanding attention with a confident presence. With a welcoming smile, he begins to address the assembled team, setting the tone for the day's meeting.

"Ladies and gentlemen, good morning. I trust you're all feeling energized and ready for a productive session ahead. Today, we gather to delve into a topic of utmost significance to our organization's success: understanding team dynamics through a strengths-based approach."

Taking a moment to allow his words to sink in, the CEO continues, "Let's embark on this journey together, exploring the intricacies of team dynamics and how we can harness the power of individual strengths to drive collective success."

With a click of a remote, the first slide of the presentation appears on the screen behind him, outlining the agenda for the meeting. "To begin, let's delve into the importance of understanding team dynamics and the foundational principles of our strengths-based approach."

As he navigates through the slides, the CEO elaborates on each point with clarity and precision. "Foundations of team dynamics are crucial for our understanding of how our teams operate and what factors influence their performance. It's about recognizing the intricate web of interactions and influences that shape our collective efforts."

Moving on to the next section, the CEO shifts his focus to individual strengths. "Each member of our team brings a unique set of strengths to the table. By identifying and recognizing these strengths, we can unlock the full potential of our team and foster a culture of empowerment and collaboration."

Transitioning seamlessly to the topic of leveraging strengths in team settings, the CEO emphasizes the importance of building complementary teams and fostering a culture of trust and accountability. "When we harness the collective power of our strengths, we can achieve remarkable results. It's about creating an environment where every team member feels valued and empowered to contribute their best."

As the CEO progresses through the agenda, he provides real-world examples and case studies to illustrate key concepts, making the material relatable and engaging for the audience. "These examples demonstrate the transformative impact of a strengths-based approach on team performance and collaboration."

As the CEO wraps up his detailed discussion on understanding team dynamics through strengths, he senses the need to delve deeper into the topic before drawing his conclusions. With a slight pause, he gathers his thoughts, ready to provide further insights to enrich the team's understanding.

"Before we conclude, I want to emphasize the importance of

CHAPTER SEVEN: LEVERAGING STRENGTHS FOR TEAM PERFORMANCE

delving into team dynamics through the lens of strengths," the CEO begins, his voice commanding attention as he addresses the assembled team. "Understanding how each team member's strengths contribute to the overall dynamics can be a game-changer in maximizing team performance and collaboration."

The room falls silent, the directors leaning forward attentively, eager to absorb the CEO's additional insights.

"We must recognize that each team is unique, comprised of individuals with diverse strengths and perspectives," the CEO continues, his tone thoughtful and deliberate. "By identifying and leveraging these strengths effectively, we can unlock the full potential of our teams and achieve greater synergy in our collective efforts."

Director Smith, known for his analytical mind, raises his hand, seeking clarification. "How can we ensure that we're effectively leveraging the strengths of each team member to optimize team dynamics?" he asks, his voice reflecting a genuine desire for practical strategies.

The CEO nods in acknowledgment of Director Smith's question, recognizing its significance in driving team effectiveness. "Optimizing team dynamics begins with fostering open communication and collaboration," he responds, his words resonating with wisdom and experience. "By encouraging dialogue and feedback, we can create an environment where each team member feels valued and empowered to contribute their unique strengths."

Director Johnson, known for her empathetic leadership style, seeks guidance on nurturing team cohesion. "What steps can we take to cultivate a sense of trust and camaraderie among team members?" she inquires, her tone conveying a genuine concern for fostering a supportive team culture.

The CEO listens attentively to Director Johnson's question, recognizing the importance of trust in building strong team dynamics. "Cultivating trust requires transparency, accountability, and empathy," he explains, his words infused with warmth and understanding. "By fostering an environment where team members feel safe to express themselves and take calculated risks, we can nurture a culture of trust and collaboration."

Director Garcia, known for her strategic insight, seeks clarification on aligning team strengths with organizational goals. "How can we ensure that our team's strengths are aligned with our broader organizational objectives?" she asks, her tone reflecting a desire for strategic direction.

The CEO considers Director Garcia's question thoughtfully, recognizing its importance in driving alignment and focus. "Aligning team strengths with organizational goals requires a clear understanding of both individual and collective strengths," he responds, his words resonating with clarity and purpose. "By setting SMART goals and regularly assessing progress, we can ensure that our teams are working towards shared objectives in a cohesive and effective manner."

With the directors' questions addressed comprehensively, the CEO prepares to offer his concluding remarks on the topic. "As we continue to navigate the complexities of team dynamics, let us remain committed to fostering a culture of collaboration, trust, and innovation," he asserts, his voice resonating with conviction and resolve. "Together, we can harness the power of our collective strengths to drive organizational success and achieve our shared goals."

With a renewed sense of clarity and purpose, the team concludes the session, empowered by their collective insights and ready to apply their understanding of team dynamics through strengths to enhance their collaborative efforts and drive organizational excellence.

In the final section of the presentation, the CEO brings everything together with a recap of key points and a call to action for applying the strengths-based approach in their daily work. "Let's seize this opportunity to leverage our strengths and drive positive change within our teams and organization. Together, we can achieve remarkable results and propel our organization to new heights."

With a sense of anticipation for the possibilities ahead, the CEO concludes the presentation, signaling the start of a dynamic discussion and exploration of team dynamics through a strengths-based lens.

As the CEO's lecture draws to a close at 12:00 PM, the anticipation in the room is intense. With a nod from the CEO, the team members rise from their seats, their minds buzzing with newfound insights and ideas. Conversations hum with excitement as colleagues exchange thoughts and reflections on the presentation.

With the morning session concluded, the team eagerly makes their way to the breakroom for lunch. The air is filled with the aroma of freshly prepared meals, and the clinking of cutlery adds to the lively atmosphere.

Amidst the chatter and laughter, team members grab their lunches and find seats around the table. Some opt for casual conversations about the morning's discussion, while others delve into deeper discussions about how they can apply the principles of understanding team dynamics through strengths in their own work.

The CEO watches with satisfaction as the team members

engage with one another, their enthusiasm for learning and growth evident in their animated conversations. It's a moment of friendship and connection, as colleagues bond over shared experiences and aspirations for the future.

As they enjoy their meal together, the team members are invigorated by the CEO's lecture, eager to return to the boardroom and continue their exploration of team dynamics through a strengths-based approach. With renewed energy and purpose, they savor this brief respite before diving back into the afternoon session.

The clock strikes 1:00 PM, and the team gathers once more, anticipation buzzing in the air. The CEO stands, ready to delve into the intricacies of building high-performing teams with complementary strengths. With a commanding presence, the CEO begins:

"Welcome back, everyone. I trust you had a rejuvenating break. Now, let's delve into the backbone of organizational success: high-performing teams."

A hush falls over the room as the CEO continues, voice resonating with authority and enthusiasm:

"Firstly, let's understand why high-performing teams are the cornerstone of any thriving organization. Their importance cannot be overstated. They are the driving force behind innovation, productivity, and ultimately, success."

Eyes fixed on the CEO, the team leans in, eager to absorb every word of wisdom.

"Next, we'll explore the essence of building teams with complementary strengths. Understanding the composition of these teams is crucial. It's not just about throwing together a group of individuals; it's about crafting a symphony of talents that harmonize to achieve greatness."

The CEO's words echo in the room, each syllable carrying weight and significance.

"We'll dissect the very fabric of high-performing teams—what makes them tick, the vital components that set them apart from the rest. Complementary strengths play a pivotal role in this dynamic, ensuring that each member brings something unique to the table."

The team nods in agreement, recognizing the truth in the CEO's words.

"Moving on, we'll explore the intricate process of identifying individual strengths. From robust assessment methods to embracing the diversity of strengths within the team, every facet contributes to the tapestry of success."

The CEO's passion is deep, igniting a spark within each team member as they hang on to every word.

"And then comes the art of creating complementary teams—matching individual strengths to team roles, striking a delicate balance between strengths and weaknesses, and employing strategies to foster cohesion."

The room buzzes with energy, team members exchanging knowing glances as they envision the possibilities ahead.

"Fostering collaboration and communication is the lifeblood of high-performing teams. Establishing clear channels, nurturing a culture of collaboration, and fostering open dialogue are imperative."

The CEO's words reverberate with conviction, driving home the importance of effective communication in team dynamics.

"Finally, we'll explore how to leverage team dynamics for unparalleled performance. From utilizing strengths to achieve collective goals to navigating challenges with resilience and determination, every step paves the way for success."

With a sense of unity and purpose, the team absorbs the CEO's insights, ready to embark on the journey of building high-performing teams.

As the CEO prepares to conclude his discussion on building high-performing teams with complementary strengths, he senses the need to provide further elaboration to ensure the team's understanding is comprehensive. With a poised demeanor, he addresses the attentive audience, ready to delve deeper into the intricacies of team dynamics.

"Before we wrap up, I believe it's essential to explore the concept of building high-performing teams with complementary strengths in greater detail," the CEO begins, his voice carrying an air of authority and expertise. "Understanding how to effectively leverage the diverse strengths of team members is crucial in fostering collaboration and achieving outstanding results."

The room falls silent, the directors leaning in attentively, eager to absorb the CEO's insights and guidance.

"Building high-performing teams begins with recognizing and valuing the unique strengths that each team member brings to the table," the CEO continues, his words infused with wisdom and experience. "By assembling a diverse team with complementary strengths, we can capitalize on a wide range of perspectives and skills, leading to enhanced creativity, problem-solving, and innovation."

Director Smith, known for his analytical mindset, raises his hand, seeking clarification on how to identify and leverage complementary strengths within a team. "How can we ensure that our team members' strengths complement each other effectively?" he asks, his tone reflecting a genuine desire for practical strategies.

CHAPTER SEVEN: LEVERAGING STRENGTHS FOR TEAM PERFORMANCE

The CEO nods appreciatively at Director Smith's question, acknowledging its importance in driving team effectiveness. "Identifying complementary strengths requires a thorough understanding of each team member's unique abilities and preferences," he explains, his words resonating with clarity and insight. "By conducting strengths assessments and facilitating open dialogue, we can pinpoint areas of overlap and synergy, allowing us to strategically allocate roles and responsibilities to maximize team performance."

Director Johnson, known for her empathetic leadership style, seeks guidance on fostering a collaborative team culture. "How can we promote collaboration and synergy among team members with diverse strengths?" she inquires, her tone conveying a genuine concern for nurturing teamwork.

The CEO listens attentively to Director Johnson's question, recognizing the importance of fostering a supportive team environment. "Promoting collaboration begins with creating a culture of trust, respect, and open communication," he responds, his words imbued with warmth and encouragement. "By encouraging active listening, sharing feedback, and celebrating achievements, we can cultivate a sense of camaraderie and unity among team members, enabling them to leverage their complementary strengths effectively."

Director Garcia, known for her strategic insight, seeks clarification on aligning team strengths with organizational goals. "How can we ensure that our team's strengths are aligned with our broader organizational objectives?" she asks, her tone reflecting a desire for strategic alignment.

The CEO considers Director Garcia's question thoughtfully, recognizing its significance in driving alignment and focus. "Aligning team strengths with organizational goals requires a strategic approach and clear communication," he explains, his words resonating with clarity and purpose. "By establishing SMART goals, regularly assessing progress, and providing ongoing support and resources, we can ensure that our teams are working towards shared objectives in a cohesive and coordinated manner."

With the directors' questions addressed comprehensively, the CEO prepares to offer his concluding remarks on the topic. "As we continue to build high-performing teams with complementary strengths, let us remain committed to fostering collaboration, innovation, and excellence," he asserts, his voice resonating with conviction and resolve. "Together, we can harness the collective power of our diverse strengths to drive organizational success and achieve our shared goals."

With a renewed sense of clarity and purpose, the team concludes the session, empowered by their collective insights and ready to apply their understanding of building high-performing teams with complementary strengths to enhance their collaborative efforts and drive organizational excellence.

"As we conclude, remember that the path to success begins with building strong, cohesive teams. Let's heed the call to action, armed with knowledge and determination, and pave the way for unparalleled achievements."

With those final words, the CEO leaves an indelible mark on the hearts and minds of the team, setting the stage for a future brimming with promise and possibility.

"it's time for a well-deserved break. Let's take a moment to recharge and refuel before we dive back into our discussions." Announces the CEO.

A collective murmur of agreement ripples through the room as weary smiles grace the faces of the team members. They

CHAPTER SEVEN: LEVERAGING STRENGTHS FOR TEAM PERFORMANCE

exchange nods and gestures of friendship, acknowledging the CEO's thoughtful gesture.

"We've covered a lot of ground already, and I'm proud of the engagement and enthusiasm I've seen from each of you," the CEO continues, pride evident in their tone.

As anticipation fills the air, the CEO's words bring a sense of unity and purpose to the room, reminding everyone of the collective journey they're on together.

"So, take this time to relax, grab a refreshment, and perhaps engage in some casual conversation with your colleagues. We'll reconvene shortly to continue our discussions," the CEO concludes, a warm smile gracing their lips.

With that, the room erupts into motion as team members rise from their seats, stretching their limbs and exchanging lighthearted banter. The sound of laughter and clinking cups fills the air as they make their way to the refreshment area, grateful for the opportunity to recharge before the next chapter unfolds.

As the clock strikes 4:00 PM, the team members gather once again, their anticipation palpable as they await the wisdom to be imparted by the CEO. With a commanding presence, the CEO takes the stage, his demeanor exuding authority and purpose.

"Good afternoon, everyone," he begins, his voice resonating with conviction. "In this session, we embark on a journey to explore the strategies for maximizing team effectiveness."

In the introductory segment, the CEO lays the groundwork, highlighting the critical importance of team effectiveness in achieving organizational success. "Our ability to work together cohesively as a team is paramount," he asserts. "Let us delve into the strategies that will enable us to harness the full potential of our collective efforts."

With a seamless transition, the CEO delves into the first strategy: building a strong foundation. "To maximize team effectiveness, we must first establish clear goals and objectives," he explains. "By defining roles and responsibilities and fostering trust and communication, we lay the groundwork for success."

Moving forward, the CEO emphasizes the significance of leveraging diversity and inclusion within the team. "Embracing the diverse perspectives and backgrounds of our team members is key," he declares. "By creating an inclusive culture and leveraging each individual's strengths, we unlock innovation and creativity."

With unwavering focus, the CEO proceeds to discuss the importance of promoting collaboration and communication. "Open dialogue and idea sharing are essential for fostering a culture of collaboration," he affirms. "Through effective communication channels and a shared commitment to teamwork, we amplify our collective impact."

As the discussion progresses, the CEO guides the team through the strategies for setting and monitoring progress, providing support and development, and resolving conflicts. "By establishing measurable goals, offering continuous support, and addressing conflicts constructively, we strengthen our team's resilience and adaptability," he explains.

In the penultimate segment, the CEO underscores the significance of celebrating successes and recognizing contributions. "Acknowledging achievements and fostering a culture of appreciation are essential for morale and motivation," he states. "Let us never underestimate the power of recognition in fueling our team's success."

CHAPTER SEVEN: LEVERAGING STRENGTHS FOR TEAM PERFORMANCE

With a resounding call to action, the CEO concludes the lecture, leaving the team inspired and empowered to implement the strategies for maximizing team effectiveness. "Together, let us commit to implementing these strategies with diligence and dedication," he declares. "For it is through our collective efforts that we will achieve greatness."

As the CEO concludes the final lecture of the day, a sense of accomplishment fills the room. The team members exchange satisfied smiles, knowing they've gained invaluable insights that will propel them forward.

"Well, team, that wraps up our sessions for today. I want to thank each and every one of you for your unwavering attention and active participation." States the CEO with a smile.

The CEO's words are met with nods of appreciation and murmurs of agreement from the team.

"It's been a fruitful day, filled with rich discussions and invaluable learnings. I'm truly impressed by the dedication and enthusiasm I've witnessed." Continues the CEO with gratitude.

A ripple of applause breaks out, echoing the team's appreciation for the CEO's leadership and guidance throughout the day.

"Now, I don't know about you, but I think we've earned ourselves a well-deserved rest. Let's reconvene tomorrow morning, bright and early, and continue our journey toward success." Says the CEO with a touch of humor.

With a final nod of encouragement, the CEO gestures toward the door, signaling the end of the day's proceedings.

"Until then, take some time to recharge and reflect on everything we've discussed. I have no doubt that with our collective effort and determination, we'll achieve great things together. Goodbye for now and see you all bright and early tomorrow." Concludes the CEO with a sense of pride.

As the team members begin to file out of the room, a sense of camaraderie and excitement lingers in the air. They know that tomorrow brings new challenges and opportunities, but they're ready to face them head-on, armed with the knowledge and inspiration gained from today's sessions.

8

Chapter Eight: Developing Strengths-Based Talent Management Practices

As the clock strikes 9:00 AM on Thursday morning, the conference room buzz with anticipation. Participants filter in, their chatter gradually hushing as they take their seats. The atmosphere crackle with energy, a deep sense of eagerness filling the air.

At the front of the room, the CEO, a figure of authority and charisma, stands poised behind the podium. With a confident smile, he surveys the room, his eyes alight with purpose. As the last few stragglers settle in, he clears his throat, commanding the attention of all present.

"Good morning, everyone," his voice boom, commanding respect and attention. "Welcome to our annual recruitment and selection conference. Today marks a pivotal moment in our journey towards excellence, as we come together to explore new strategies and approaches."

With a graceful gesture, he motions towards the Director of

Human Resources, a figure of poise and expertise, standing beside him. "Without further ado, I'll hand over to our esteemed Director of Human Resources, who will guide us through the importance of integrating strengths in our recruitment and selection processes."

The Director steps forward, her presence commanding the room with quiet authority. He adjusts his glasses, his demeanor exuding confidence and knowledge. Taking a deep breath, he begins to speak, his words carrying weight and significance.

"Thank you, CEO, and good morning, everyone," he begins, his voice steady and assured. "Today, we embark on a journey towards a more effective and impactful approach to recruitment and selection. At the heart of this journey lies the concept of integrating strengths."

With precision and clarity, he delves into the intricacies of integrating strengths into the recruitment process, painting a vivid picture of its importance and relevance. His words flow like a river, carrying the audience along on a journey of enlightenment and discovery.

As he speaks, heads nod in understanding, murmurs of agreement rippling through the room. Eyes sparkled with newfound insight, minds racing with possibilities. In his hands, the topic transformed from a mere concept into a tangible strategy, ripe with potential.

By the time he concludes his remarks, the room was buzzing with excitement and enthusiasm. The participants exchange eager glances, their minds buzzing with ideas and possibilities. Under the guidance of their visionary leaders, they are ready to revolutionize their approach to recruitment and selection, armed with the power of integrated strengths.

As the Director of Human Resources continues his address,

his words carried a weight of purpose and innovation that filled the room like a gust of wind. With each syllable, he weaves a tapestry of possibilities, painting a vivid picture of a future where strengths were not just acknowledged, but celebrated and integrated into every facet of talent management.

"Imagine," he begins, his voice resonating with passion and conviction, "a workplace where every individual's strengths are not only recognized but embraced as essential assets to our collective success. This vision extends far beyond mere recruitment; it encompasses every stage of talent management, from onboarding to career development."

His words hung in the air, stirring something deep within each listener, igniting a spark of inspiration that threatens to blaze into a wildfire of transformation. He paces the stage, his movements purposeful and deliberate, his gaze locking onto each participant with unwavering intensity.

"We must engage our directors in discussions," he declares, his voice ringing with authority, "on how to infuse strengths-based practices into every aspect of our talent management processes. Recruitment, onboarding, career development—they are not isolated endeavors, but interconnected threads in the rich tapestry of our organizational culture."

As he speaks, the room seems to pulsate with energy, the very air crackling with anticipation. Minds race with possibilities, imaginations running wild with the promise of a future where individual strengths were aligned seamlessly with organizational goals and objectives.

"We must explore ways," he continues, his words a rallying cry for change, "to forge a symbiotic relationship between individual strengths and organizational objectives. Only then can we unlock the true potential of our workforce, unleashing a torrent of innovation and excellence that knows no bounds."

His message resonates deeply with each listener, striking a chord that reverberated through the very foundation of their beliefs. In his hands, the concept of integrating strengths into talent management ceased to be a mere idea—it becomes a rallying cry, a call to arms for a brighter, more prosperous future.

As James, concludes his detailed discussion on integrating strengths into recruitment and selection, he opens the floor to the directors, eager to address any lingering questions or insights they may have. With a sense of anticipation, he welcomes their inquiries, ready to engage in a fruitful dialogue to ensure clarity and understanding among the team.

"Before we wrap up, I'd like to invite any questions or thoughts you may have regarding the integration of strengths into recruitment and selection," James announces, his tone reflecting both confidence and receptiveness.

Director Smith, known for his analytical approach, raises his hand, indicating his readiness to delve deeper into the topic. "How do we identify and assess strengths during the recruitment process, especially when candidates may not have prior work experience?" he asks, his tone conveying a genuine desire for practical solutions.

James nods appreciatively at Director Smith's question, acknowledging its importance in selecting candidates who are the best fit for the organization. "Identifying and assessing strengths in candidates without prior work experience requires a holistic approach," he responds, his words reflecting a blend of experience and insight. "By leveraging tools such as behavioral assessments, situational judgment tests, and structured interviews, we can gain valuable insights into candidates' strengths, values, and potential fit within our organization."

Director Johnson, known for her empathetic leadership style, seeks clarification on fostering inclusivity in the recruitment process. "How do we ensure that our recruitment practices are inclusive and equitable, allowing candidates from diverse backgrounds to showcase their strengths?" she asks, her tone reflecting a genuine concern for promoting diversity and fairness.

James listens attentively to Director Johnson's question, recognizing the importance of fostering an inclusive recruitment process. "Promoting inclusivity in recruitment requires creating standardized processes, minimizing biases, and providing opportunities for candidates to demonstrate their strengths," he explains, his words resonating with empathy and understanding. "By ensuring transparency, offering diverse interview panels, and providing accommodations where needed, we can create a level playing field where all candidates have the opportunity to shine."

Director Garcia, known for her strategic insight, seeks guidance on aligning recruitment strategies with organizational culture. "How do we ensure that our recruitment efforts align with our organizational values and culture, attracting candidates who embody our desired strengths?" she asks, her tone reflecting a desire for strategic alignment.

James considers Director Garcia's question thoughtfully, acknowledging its significance in building a cohesive team culture. "Aligning recruitment strategies with organizational culture requires defining our core values, communicating them effectively, and integrating them into our recruitment process," he responds, his words infused with clarity and purpose. "By showcasing our values in job postings, assessing candidates for cultural fit, and involving current employees in the selection process, we can attract candidates who share our values and contribute to our organizational culture."

Director Patel, known for his innovative approach, seeks guidance on leveraging technology in the recruitment process. "How can we use technology to streamline our recruitment efforts and identify candidates with the right strengths more efficiently?" he asks, his tone reflecting a desire for efficiency and effectiveness.

James listens attentively to Director Patel's question, recognizing the potential of technology to enhance the recruitment process. "Leveraging technology in recruitment requires leveraging applicant tracking systems, artificial intelligence, and predictive analytics," he explains, his words imbued with enthusiasm and innovation. "By automating repetitive tasks, analyzing data to identify trends, and using algorithms to match candidates with job requirements, we can streamline our recruitment efforts and identify candidates with the right strengths more efficiently."

With the directors' questions addressed comprehensively, James prepares to offer his concluding remarks on the topic. "As we conclude our discussion on integrating strengths into recruitment and selection, let us remain committed to attracting, selecting, and retaining top talent who embody our organizational values and strengths," he asserts, his voice resonating with conviction and resolve. "Together, we can build a high-performing team that drives organizational success and achieves our shared goals."

With a renewed sense of purpose and understanding, the team concludes the session, empowered by their collective insights and ready to apply their understanding of integrating strengths into recruitment and selection to enhance their hiring practices and build a stronger organization.

As the clock strikes noon, the conference room hummed with anticipation, the morning's discussions still echoing in the minds of the participants. Tension ebbs as the CEO rose once more, his commanding presence bringing a sense of order to the room.

"Ladies and gentlemen," he announces, his voice cutting through the air like a clarion call, "it is now time for a well-deserved break. Let us reconvene at 1:00 PM, refreshed and ready to continue our journey towards excellence."

With a nod of approval, he signals the end of the morning session, and the room erupts into motion. Chairs scraped against the floor as participants rise from their seats, eager chatter filling the air like a symphony of anticipation.

Amidst the bustling crowd, friendships forged and alliances strengthened as colleagues exchange pleasantries and share insights from the morning's discussions. Laughter mingled with animated conversation, creating a vibrant tapestry of friendship and collaboration.

Outside the conference room, the aroma of freshly prepared food waft through the air, beckoning the participants to the nearby buffet. Excited chatter fills the hallway as they line up, plates in hand, eager to indulge in a well-deserved feast.

As they savor each bite, their minds wander back to the morning's revelations, thoughts swirling with possibilities and potential. Energized and invigorated, they eagerly await the afternoon session, eager to continue their exploration of integrating strengths into every aspect of talent management.

With satisfied smiles and renewed determination, they vow

to make the most of the lunch break, savoring not only the delicious food but also the bonds of friendship and collaboration forged in the crucible of shared purpose.

And as the clock tick away the minutes, marking the passage of time, they know that they are not just breaking for lunch—they were breaking barriers, forging new paths towards a future where strengths were not just acknowledged, but celebrated and integrated into every facet of their professional lives.

As the clock strikes 1:00 PM, the room falls into a hushed reverence, the anticipation intense as participants settle into their seats once more. At the forefront stands the director, a beacon of knowledge and guidance amidst eager gazes.

With a commanding presence, the director begins to lecture on the vital subject of training and development for strengths enhancement. Their voice carries the weight of authority as they delve into the intricacies of the topic.

"In our journey of growth and empowerment," the director begins, "training and development serve as the foundation upon which we build our strengths." Each word is deliberate, setting the stage for what is to come.

The director paints a vivid picture of the importance of strengths enhancement, emphasizing its role in personal and professional success. "Our strengths are not merely attributes; they are the catalysts for excellence," they proclaim, their passion igniting a fire within the audience.

As the lecture progresses, the director guides the participants through a journey of self-discovery, encouraging them to identify their individual strengths and recognize the value of leveraging them to their fullest potential.

They delve into various training methods, from assessment tools for identifying strengths to tailoring programs to individual needs. "Experiential learning is key," the director emphasizes, "for it is through experience that we truly internalize and refine our strengths."

Development strategies are explored in depth, with the director urging the audience to cultivate a growth mindset and seek mentorship and coaching opportunities to aid in their journey of self-improvement.

The integration of strengths enhancement into organizational culture is highlighted as crucial, with the director stressing the importance of fostering a strengths-based approach and aligning individual strengths with organizational goals.

As the lecture draws to a close, the director leaves the audience with a sense of purpose and determination. "Let us embrace this journey of strengths enhancement," they exclaim, "for it is through our commitment and dedication that we will achieve greatness."

As James, wraps up his comprehensive discussion on training and development for strengths enhancement, he opens the floor to the directors, eager to address any lingering questions or insights they may have. With a sense of anticipation, he welcomes their inquiries, ready to engage in a fruitful dialogue to ensure clarity and understanding among the team.

"Before we conclude, I'd like to invite any questions or thoughts you may have regarding training and development for strengths enhancement," James announces, his tone reflecting both confidence and receptiveness.

Director Smith, known for his analytical approach, raises his hand, indicating his readiness to delve deeper into the topic. "How do we tailor training programs to accommodate different learning styles and preferences, ensuring that each employee can effectively enhance their strengths?" he asks, his tone conveying a genuine desire for practical solutions.

James nods appreciatively at Director Smith's question, acknowledging its importance in designing effective training initiatives. "Tailoring training programs to accommodate diverse learning styles requires a multi-faceted approach," he responds, his words reflecting a blend of experience and insight. "By offering a variety of learning modalities such as workshops, online courses, mentorship programs, and hands-on experiences, we can cater to the individual preferences and needs of our employees, facilitating optimal strengths enhancement."

Director Johnson, known for her empathetic leadership style, seeks clarification on fostering inclusivity in training and development initiatives. "How do we ensure that our training programs are inclusive and accessible to employees from diverse backgrounds, allowing everyone to participate and thrive?" she asks, her tone reflecting a genuine concern for promoting diversity and equity.

James listens attentively to Director Johnson's question, recognizing the importance of fostering an inclusive learning environment. "Promoting inclusivity in training and development requires creating accessible materials, providing accommodations where needed, and fostering a culture of respect and acceptance," he explains, his words resonating with empathy and understanding. "By offering flexible scheduling, providing language support, and incorporating diverse perspectives into our training content, we can create an inclusive learning environment where all employees feel valued and supported in their strengths enhancement journey."

Director Garcia, known for her strategic insight, seeks guidance on measuring the effectiveness of training initiatives.

"How do we assess the impact of our training and development programs on strengths enhancement, ensuring that they are achieving the desired outcomes?" she asks, her tone reflecting a desire for strategic alignment and accountability.

James considers Director Garcia's question thoughtfully, acknowledging the importance of evaluating training effectiveness. "Assessing the impact of training and development programs requires establishing clear objectives, collecting feedback from participants, and measuring outcomes against predetermined metrics," he responds, his words infused with clarity and purpose. "By conducting pre-and post-training assessments, tracking performance improvements, and soliciting employee feedback, we can evaluate the effectiveness of our programs and make data-driven decisions to continuously enhance strengths development initiatives."

Director Patel, known for his innovative approach, seeks guidance on leveraging technology in training and development efforts. "How can we leverage technology to enhance the delivery and accessibility of training programs, ensuring that employees can access resources and support anytime, anywhere?" he asks, his tone reflecting a desire for efficiency and effectiveness.

James listens attentively to Director Patel's question, recognizing the potential of technology to enhance learning experiences. "Leveraging technology in training and development requires utilizing e-learning platforms, virtual reality simulations, and mobile applications," he explains, his words imbued with enthusiasm and innovation. "By offering on-demand access to training materials, creating interactive learning experiences, and incorporating gamification elements, we can engage employees more effectively and empower them to enhance their strengths at their own pace and convenience."

With the directors' questions addressed comprehensively, James prepares to offer his concluding remarks on training and development for strengths enhancement. "As we conclude our discussion on training and development, let us remain committed to providing our employees with the resources, support, and opportunities they need to enhance their strengths and achieve their full potential," he asserts, his voice resonating with conviction and resolve. "Together, we can build a culture of continuous learning and growth that drives individual and organizational success."

With a renewed sense of purpose and understanding, the team concludes the session, empowered by their collective insights and ready to apply their understanding of training and development for strengths enhancement to drive organizational growth and success

In the end, the room is charged with energy and possibility, as each participant commits to forging their own path towards a strengths-focused future.

After a refreshing tea break, the participants reconvene promptly at 4:00 PM, their energy renewed and focus sharpened for the continuation of the day's proceedings. The director resumes their position at the front of the room, a beacon of knowledge amidst the eager audience.

"With our minds invigorated and spirits renewed, let us delve deeper into the realm of Performance Management and Recognition based on Strengths," declares the director, their voice commanding attention.

In the introductory segment, the director elucidates the essence of performance management, meticulously defining its role in organizational success. "Performance management," they articulate, "is not merely a process but a strategic endeavor aimed at maximizing individual and collective potential."

Transitioning seamlessly, the director emphasizes the paramount importance of recognizing and leveraging strengths within the framework of performance management. "Our strengths," they assert, "are not to be overlooked but celebrated and harnessed as catalysts for excellence."

As the lecture progresses, the director navigates through the labyrinth of identifying individual strengths, illuminating assessment tools and techniques to unveil the unique abilities inherent within each employee. "To truly harness the power of strengths," they declare, "we must first recognize and acknowledge them."

In the subsequent segment, the director delves into the intricacies of performance management systems, weaving together strategies to integrate strengths-based approaches into evaluations and goal-setting processes. "Aligning performance goals with individual strengths," they emphasize, "is paramount for fostering engagement and driving performance."

With fervor, the director unveils a tapestry of recognition strategies, each thread meticulously designed to celebrate and reinforce strengths-based achievements. "Recognition," they proclaim, "is not merely a formality but a powerful motivator that fuels individual growth and organizational success."

Transitioning seamlessly, the director elucidates the importance of developing strengths, offering a plethora of opportunities for training, application, and growth. "Continuous learning and growth," they affirm, "are the cornerstones of a thriving organizational culture."

In the penultimate segment, the director paints a vision of integration into organizational culture, fostering a nurturing environment where strengths-based practices flourish and align seamlessly with overarching values and goals.

As James invites questions from the directors regarding training and development for strengths enhancement, the room fills with anticipation, each director eager to contribute to the discussion and gain further clarity on the topic.

Director Smith, known for his analytical mindset, is the first to raise his hand. "James, can you elaborate on how we can tailor training programs to accommodate different learning styles and preferences?" he inquires, his tone reflecting a genuine interest in practical implementation.

James nods appreciatively at Director Smith's question, acknowledging its significance in crafting effective training initiatives. "Certainly, Smith," he responds, his voice projecting confidence and expertise. "We can customize training programs by offering a variety of learning modalities such as workshops, online courses, and mentorship programs to cater to the diverse learning preferences of our employees."

Director Johnson, renowned for her empathetic leadership style, raises her hand next, her eyes reflecting a desire for inclusivity. "How do we ensure that our training programs are accessible to employees from diverse backgrounds?" she asks, her voice carrying a note of empathy.

James listens attentively to Director Johnson's inquiry, recognizing the importance of fostering inclusivity in training initiatives. "Inclusivity in training programs involves creating accessible materials, providing accommodations, and fostering a culture of respect and acceptance," he explains, his words imbued with empathy and understanding.

Director Garcia, known for her strategic acumen, poses a question about measuring the effectiveness of training initiatives. "James, how do we assess the impact of our training programs on strengths enhancement?" she queries, her tone reflecting a desire for accountability and strategic alignment.

James considers Director Garcia's question thoughtfully, emphasizing the importance of evaluating training effectiveness. "Assessing the impact of training programs requires establishing clear objectives, collecting feedback, and measuring outcomes against predetermined metrics," he responds, his words resonating with clarity and purpose.

Director Patel, renowned for his innovative thinking, raises a question about leveraging technology in training efforts. "James, how can we use technology to enhance the delivery and accessibility of our training programs?" he asks, his tone reflecting a desire for efficiency and effectiveness.

James nods approvingly at Director Patel's question, recognizing the potential of technology in enhancing learning experiences. "Leveraging technology involves utilizing e-learning platforms, virtual reality simulations, and mobile applications to provide on-demand access to training materials and create interactive learning experiences," he explains, his words infused with enthusiasm and innovation.

With the directors' questions addressed comprehensively, James prepares to offer his concluding remarks on training and development for strengths enhancement, confident in the team's collective understanding and readiness to drive organizational growth and success.

Finally, as the lecture draws to a close, the director offers a heartfelt conclusion, recapitulating key concepts and championing an ongoing commitment to leveraging strengths in performance management and recognition. "Let us," they implore, "forge ahead with unwavering resolve, towards a future where every individual's strengths are celebrated, nurtured, and unleashed to their fullest potential."

As the discussion winds down and the energy in the room begins to settle, all eyes turn to the CEO, the beacon of leadership at the head of the table. With a gentle but commanding presence, they rise to their feet, their expression one of gratitude and respect.

"My esteemed colleagues," the CEO begins, their voice carrying weight and warmth in equal measure, "as we draw this meeting to a close, I want to take a moment to express my sincere gratitude to each and every one of you."

The room falls into a reverent silence, each participant leaning in to catch the CEO's words, their attention unwavering.

"Your dedication, your insights, and your unwavering commitment to our shared vision are what make this organization truly exceptional," the CEO continues, their words resonating with authenticity.

With a sweep of their hand, the CEO gestures to encompass the entire room, acknowledging the collective effort that has brought them together.

"I want to thank you for your contributions, for your passion, and for your unwavering dedication to excellence," they say, their gaze sweeping across the faces of those gathered.

"In every idea shared, in every challenge overcome, and in every milestone achieved, it is your hard work and your unwavering commitment that propel us forward," the CEO declares, their voice ringing with sincerity.

As they bring their remarks to a close, the CEO's gratitude fills the room like a warm embrace, enveloping each participant in a sense of appreciation and belonging.

"Thank you," they say simply, their words carrying the weight of genuine appreciation. "Thank you for everything."

And with those heartfelt words, the CEO brings the meeting to a close, leaving behind a lingering sense of camaraderie and shared purpose that will carry them forward into the days ahead.

9

Chapter Nine: Leading Change with a Strength-Based Approach

In the tranquil ambiance of his office, the CEO sits poised behind his desk, the morning sunlight filtering through the windows, casting a warm glow upon the room. With focused determination, he sifts through reports and plans, preparing for the day ahead.

Suddenly, the serene atmosphere is interrupted by the melodious chime of his phone. The CEO's attention is instantly drawn to the device, recognizing the incoming call from none other than the board chairperson—a woman of remarkable stature, adorned with a wealth of experience and wisdom garnered from her illustrious career in both the public and private sectors.

With a sense of anticipation, the CEO swiftly answers the call, his voice tinged with respect and admiration as he greets the esteemed chairperson. "Good morning, Madam chairperson," he says, his tone conveying deference and professionalism.

On the other end of the line, the chairperson's voice exudes an air of authority and sophistication, her words measured yet

CHAPTER NINE: LEADING CHANGE WITH A STRENGTH-BASED APPROACH

commanding as she initiates the conversation. "Good morning, CEO," she responds, her voice resonating with a quiet power that demands attention.

Inquiring about the imminent quarterly board meeting, the chairperson demonstrates her meticulous attention to detail and her unwavering commitment to the organization's governance. With precision, she seeks clarification on agenda items, deadlines, and expectations, leaving no stone unturned in her quest for clarity and efficiency.

As they discuss the agenda and logistics of the upcoming meeting, the CEO finds himself captivated by the chairperson's astute insights and keen intellect. Her guidance serves as a beacon of guidance, illuminating the path forward with clarity and purpose.

In the midst of their conversation, the CEO is struck by the chairperson's grace and poise, marveling at her ability to navigate the complexities of leadership with such grace and finesse. It is a humbling reminder of the caliber of individuals who comprise the organization's leadership, each one contributing their unique talents and perspectives to the collective journey towards success.

With the call drawing to a close, the CEO expresses his gratitude to the chairperson for her invaluable input and guidance, his admiration for her unwavering leadership evident in his words. As they bid farewell, both parties are left with a renewed sense of purpose and determination, fortified by the knowledge that they are united in their shared commitment to the organization's mission and vision.

The CEO's office hums with energy as he swiftly concludes his call with the chairperson, his mind already shifting gears to the next task at hand. With purposeful strides, he moves towards the door, anticipation coursing through his veins as he prepares to greet the visitor who awaits.

Upon reaching the threshold, the CEO is met by his secretary, who delivers a timely tip about the impending arrival of their esteemed guest. With a nod of appreciation, the CEO rushes forward, his eagerness strong as he prepares to welcome the visitor.

As he steps into the reception area, his eyes fall upon a figure of grace and authority—Sibongile, the director of operations from their sister company. Her presence commands attention, exuding confidence and poise as she awaits the CEO's approach.

With a warm smile, the CEO extends his hand in greeting, his expression one of genuine pleasure at the opportunity to meet such a distinguished guest. "Sibongile, it's a pleasure to finally meet you," he says, his voice filled with warmth and sincerity.

Sibongile returns the gesture with a firm handshake, her eyes alight with enthusiasm as she reciprocates the CEO's greeting. "Likewise, CEO," she replies, her tone respectful yet assured.

As they exchange pleasantries, the CEO is struck by Sibongile's aura of professionalism and expertise. Her reputation precedes her—a seasoned leader with a wealth of knowledge and experience in operations management.

The clock strikes 9:00 AM, signaling the commencement of a pivotal moment in the conference room. The CEO, a figure of authority and leadership, stands tall at the front, his presence commanding attention. With a nod, he welcomes the assembled directors, their anticipation strong in the air.

"Ladies and gentlemen," the CEO begins, his voice resonating with authority, "today, we have the privilege of hearing from a distinguished guest—a beacon of knowledge and expertise in the realm of change management."

With a graceful gesture, the CEO introduces Sibongile, the director of operations from the sister company. Sibongile, vibrant and intelligent, exudes confidence as she steps forward to address the attentive audience.

"Thank you, CEO, for the kind introduction," Sibongile says, her voice ringing with clarity and purpose. "Today, I am honored to lead a discussion on a topic that is paramount to our collective success—Overcoming Resistance to Change."

With the room hanging on her every word, Sibongile delves into the intricacies of resistance to change, painting a vivid picture of its impact on individuals and organizational performance. "Resistance to change," she explains, "can manifest in various forms, from skepticism to outright opposition, and can pose significant challenges to our progress."

She outlines common reasons for resistance and shares insights on identifying signs within an organization. "Understanding the root causes of resistance is crucial," Sibongile emphasizes, "as it allows us to anticipate challenges and develop proactive strategies for addressing them."

Drawing from her wealth of experience, Sibongile unveils a comprehensive framework for overcoming resistance to change. She highlights the importance of communication, transparency, and involvement in engaging stakeholders and fostering a culture of collaboration.

"By providing open and honest communication, soliciting input, and offering support," she explains, "we can empower individuals to embrace change and contribute to our collective success."

As she delves into the implementation and monitoring of change initiatives, Sibongile emphasizes the need for adaptability and reflection. "Change is an ongoing process," she reminds the audience, "and it requires continuous evaluation and adjustment to ensure its success."

As Sibongile opens the floor for questions on overcoming resistance to change, the directors eagerly raise their hands, each eager to contribute their perspective and seek clarification on this critical topic.

Director Smith, known for his analytical approach, is the first to speak up. "Sibongile, how do we identify the root causes of resistance within our organization?" he asks, his tone reflecting a keen interest in understanding the underlying factors.

Sibongile nods thoughtfully at Director Smith's question, recognizing its importance in addressing resistance effectively. "Identifying the root causes of resistance involves conducting thorough stakeholder analysis, gathering feedback from employees, and assessing organizational culture," she explains, her voice conveying a sense of insight and expertise.

Director Johnson, valued for her empathetic leadership style, raises her hand next. "Sibongile, how can we support employees who are experiencing fear or uncertainty about upcoming changes?" she inquires, her tone conveying a genuine concern for employee well-being.

Sibongile listens empathetically to Director Johnson's question, acknowledging the significance of providing support during times of change. "Supporting employees during change involves fostering open communication, providing resources for skill development, and offering emotional support through coaching and counseling," she responds, her words resonating with compassion and understanding.

Director Garcia, known for her strategic mindset, poses a question about anticipating and mitigating resistance. "Sibongile, what strategies can we employ to anticipate potential sources of resistance and address them proactively?" she asks, her tone reflecting a desire for proactive problem-solving.

Sibongile considers Director Garcia's question thoughtfully, emphasizing the importance of proactive planning. "Anticipating resistance involves conducting impact assessments, engaging stakeholders early in the process, and communicating the benefits of change transparently," she explains, her words carrying a sense of strategic foresight.

Director Patel, recognized for his innovative thinking, raises a question about fostering a culture of change readiness. "Sibongile, how can we cultivate a culture that embraces change and innovation?" he queries, his tone conveying a desire for transformative leadership.

Sibongile nods approvingly at Director Patel's question, recognizing the importance of cultural alignment. "Fostering a culture of change readiness involves promoting a growth mindset, encouraging experimentation, and celebrating successes," she responds, her words infused with optimism and forward-thinking.

With the directors' questions addressed comprehensively, Sibongile prepares to offer her concluding remarks on overcoming resistance to change, confident in the team's collective understanding and commitment to driving organizational success.

In conclusion, Sibongile recaps the key strategies for overcoming resistance to change, underlining the importance of proactive and adaptive approaches. "Let us," she declares, "embrace change as an opportunity for growth and innovation, and together, we can navigate the challenges ahead with confidence and resilience."

With her final words echoing in the room, Sibongile's lecture leaves a profound impact on the audience, igniting a sense of determination and resolve to overcome resistance and drive positive change within the organization.

As the first session draws to a close, the CEO stands at the front of the room, a beacon of authority amidst the attentive audience. With a confident demeanor, he addresses the assembled group.

"Ladies and gentlemen," he begins, his voice carrying across the room with clarity and warmth, "I want to extend my gratitude to each of you for your active participation and engagement in our first session."

A collective murmur of appreciation ripples through the room, testament to the CEO's acknowledgment of the group's efforts.

"In recognition of your dedication and hard work," the CEO continues, his tone inviting, "I am pleased to announce a break for lunch."

A wave of anticipation washes over the audience, mingled with a sense of relief and excitement at the prospect of a well-deserved respite.

"I encourage you all to take this opportunity to recharge and refuel," the CEO urges, his words laced with encouragement. "We have a full agenda ahead of us, and I want each of you to return refreshed and ready for the next session."

With a gracious smile, the CEO nods, signaling the start of the break. As the room erupts into movement, participants exchange smiles and pleasantries, grateful for the chance to unwind before the afternoon's proceedings.

Amidst the chatter and laughter, the CEO's announcement echoes in the air, a reminder of the organization's commitment

CHAPTER NINE: LEADING CHANGE WITH A STRENGTH-BASED APPROACH

to fostering a supportive and inclusive environment for all. With anticipation for the sessions yet to come, the group disperses, each member eager to make the most of the lunch break and return reenergized for the remainder of the day.

As the clock strikes 1:00 PM, the team reconvenes with a sense of purpose and anticipation. The room hums with energy as they gather, eager to delve deeper into the subject at hand. Without missing a beat, she steps forward, her presence commanding attention as she resumes her lecture on "Using Strengths to drive Organizational Transformation."

"In our quest for organizational transformation," she begins, her voice resolute and assured, "it is imperative that we first understand the essence of this journey." With clarity, she defines organizational transformation as a fundamental shift in mindset, culture, and practices aimed at achieving long-term success.

Transitioning seamlessly, she introduces the concept of a strengths-based approach, emphasizing its power to drive meaningful change. "At the heart of organizational transformation lies our ability to leverage strengths," she asserts, her words igniting a spark of inspiration within the audience.

In the next segment, she delves into the intricacies of understanding strengths, urging the team to identify both individual and collective strengths within the organization. "Our strengths are the building blocks of our success," she declares, "and it is essential that we recognize their value and potential."

With purpose, she guides the team through the process of aligning strengths with organizational goals. "By assessing our objectives and vision," she explains, "we can identify opportunities to leverage strengths and establish alignment between individual and organizational aspirations."

As she transitions to implementing strengths-based strategies, she highlights the critical role of leadership development. "Empowering leaders to leverage their strengths is key," she emphasizes, "as is cultivating a culture that celebrates and harnesses the strengths of every individual."

Turning her focus to team dynamics, she underscores the importance of building high-performing teams based on complementary strengths. "Through collaboration and communication," she asserts, "we can maximize our collective potential and drive innovation."

In the realm of process improvement, she unveils strategies to capitalize on organizational strengths, streamlining workflows and increasing efficiency. "By redesigning processes with our strengths in mind," she proclaims, "we can pave the way for transformative change."

With passion and conviction, she discusses the cultivation of a strengths-based culture, fostering appreciation, recognition, and opportunities for growth. "Embedding strengths-based practices into our everyday operations," she concludes, "is the cornerstone of our journey towards organizational excellence."

As Sibongile opens the floor for questions on using strengths to drive organizational transformation, the room buzzes with anticipation. The directors, eager to delve deeper into this crucial topic, eagerly raise their hands, each poised to contribute their perspective and seek clarity.

Director Smith, known for his strategic thinking, is the first to speak up. "Sibongile, how do we effectively identify and leverage the strengths of our employees to drive meaningful change within our organization?" he asks, his tone reflecting a desire for practical insights.

Sibongile nods, acknowledging the importance of strategic alignment in leveraging strengths for transformation. "Identifying and leveraging strengths begins with conducting comprehensive assessments, fostering a culture of strengths awareness, and aligning individual strengths with organizational goals," she responds, her words resonating with clarity and purpose.

Director Johnson, valued for her empathetic leadership style, raises her hand next. "Sibongile, how can we ensure that our strengths-based approach promotes inclusivity and empowers all members of our organization?" she inquires, her tone reflecting a commitment to diversity and equity.

Sibongile listens attentively, recognizing the significance of inclusivity in driving organizational transformation. "Promoting inclusivity involves valuing diverse perspectives, providing opportunities for all employees to contribute their strengths, and creating a supportive environment where everyone feels empowered to thrive," she explains, her words imbued with a sense of inclusivity and belonging.

Director Garcia, known for her analytical mindset, poses a question about measuring the impact of strengths-based initiatives. "Sibongile, how do we evaluate the effectiveness of our strengths-based approach and ensure that it translates into tangible outcomes for our organization?" she asks, her tone reflecting a desire for data-driven insights.

Sibongile nods in agreement, acknowledging the importance of measuring impact to drive continuous improvement. "Evaluating the effectiveness of strengths-based initiatives involves establishing clear metrics, collecting relevant data, and analyzing outcomes to assess progress and inform future strategies," she responds, her words underscored by a commitment to accountability and results.

Director Patel, recognized for his innovative thinking, raises a question about overcoming resistance to change in the context of strengths-based transformation. "Sibongile, how can we address resistance to change and foster a culture that embraces strengths-based approaches?" he queries, his tone reflecting a desire for strategic guidance.

Sibongile considers Director Patel's question thoughtfully, recognizing the importance of change management in driving transformation. "Addressing resistance involves transparent communication, stakeholder engagement, and providing support for individuals to adapt to new ways of working," she explains, her words infused with a sense of resilience and adaptability.

With the directors' questions addressed comprehensively, Sibongile prepares to offer her concluding remarks on using strengths to drive organizational transformation, confident in the team's readiness to embrace change and drive meaningful progress.

As she wraps up her lecture, she leaves the team with a call to action—a call for ongoing commitment to a strengths-driven organizational culture. "Let us embrace the transformative potential of leveraging strengths," she implores, "and together, we can chart a course towards a brighter future."

After a brief interlude for tea, the team gathers once more, the anticipation deep in the air as they prepare to delve into the next phase of their meeting. With a sense of purpose, she steps forward, ready to guide them through the intricacies of "Creating a Culture of Continuous Improvement."

"As we reconvene," she begins, her voice resonating with clarity and determination, "let us embark on a journey to cultivate a culture that embraces change and innovation at every turn."

In the introductory segment, she lays the groundwork by defining continuous improvement as a relentless pursuit of excellence, driven by the collective efforts of every individual within the organization. "Continuous improvement," she explains, "is not merely a goal but a mindset—a commitment to always strive for better."

Transitioning seamlessly, she explores the significance of fostering a culture of continuous improvement, underscoring its potential to propel organizations to new heights of success. "In an ever-evolving landscape," she asserts, "those who embrace continuous improvement are better equipped to adapt, innovate, and thrive."

With passion and conviction, she delves into the principles of continuous improvement, illuminating the path forward with clarity and insight. "At its core," she declares, "continuous improvement is about challenging the status quo, seeking feedback, and never settling for mediocrity."

In the next segment, she shines a spotlight on leadership's pivotal role in driving continuous improvement, emphasizing the importance of setting the tone from the top. "Leaders," she emphasizes, "must not only champion continuous improvement but also empower employees to actively contribute to improvement efforts."

As she discusses the creation of systems and processes to support continuous improvement, she underscores the need for robust feedback mechanisms, regular performance evaluations, and ample resources for improvement initiatives. "By providing the necessary infrastructure," she explains, "we can foster an environment where continuous improvement can thrive."

Turning her attention to employee engagement and participation, she highlights the importance of creating a culture of openness, transparency, and recognition. "When employees feel valued and empowered," she asserts, "they are more likely to actively engage in continuous improvement efforts."

In the subsequent segments, she outlines strategies for implementing continuous improvement projects, evaluating their effectiveness, and sustaining a culture of continuous improvement for the long term.

As Sibongile opens the floor for questions on creating a culture of continuous improvement, the directors eagerly seize the opportunity to gain further insights into this vital aspect of organizational development. Each director, driven by a desire to foster growth and innovation within their teams, raises probing questions, eager to glean valuable insights from Sibongile's expertise.

Director Smith, renowned for his strategic vision, is the first to speak up. "Sibongile, how can we effectively instill a mindset of continuous improvement among our employees, ensuring that they are committed to seeking out and implementing opportunities for growth?" he inquires, his tone reflecting a deep-seated desire for sustainable progress.

Sibongile acknowledges the importance of cultivating a culture of continuous improvement and responds, "Instilling a mindset of continuous improvement requires clear communication of expectations, recognition of efforts, and providing resources for skill development and innovation," her words resonating with conviction and purpose.

Director Johnson, known for her empathetic leadership style, raises her hand next. "Sibongile, how can we foster psychological safety within our teams to encourage open dialogue and experimentation, essential components of a culture of continuous improvement?" she asks, her tone reflecting a commitment to nurturing a supportive work environment.

Sibongile listens attentively, recognizing the significance of psychological safety in fostering innovation and growth. "Fostering psychological safety involves promoting trust, encouraging diverse perspectives, and embracing failure as an opportunity for learning and growth," she explains, her words imbued with empathy and understanding.

Director Garcia, valued for her analytical mindset, poses a question about measuring the effectiveness of continuous improvement initiatives. "Sibongile, how do we assess the impact of our efforts to create a culture of continuous improvement and ensure that they translate into tangible outcomes for our organization?" she inquires, her tone reflecting a desire for data-driven insights.

Sibongile nods in agreement, acknowledging the importance of measuring impact to drive meaningful progress. "Assessing the impact of continuous improvement initiatives involves setting clear metrics, collecting relevant data, and analyzing outcomes to identify areas for improvement and refinement," she responds, her words underscored by a commitment to accountability and results.

Director Patel, recognized for his innovative thinking, raises a question about overcoming obstacles to continuous improvement. "Sibongile, how can we address resistance to change and overcome other barriers that may hinder our efforts to foster a culture of continuous improvement?" he queries, his tone reflecting a desire for strategic guidance.

Sibongile considers Director Patel's question thoughtfully,

recognizing the importance of resilience in navigating challenges. "Addressing resistance involves proactive communication, soliciting feedback, and providing support for individuals to adapt to new ways of working," she explains, her words infused with a sense of determination and adaptability.

With the directors' questions addressed comprehensively, Sibongile prepares to offer her concluding remarks on creating a culture of continuous improvement, confident in the team's ability to embrace change and drive meaningful progress.

As she concludes her lecture, she leaves the team with a call to action—a call to embrace the transformative power of continuous improvement and commit to fostering a culture where innovation and growth are not just encouraged but celebrated. "Let us," she urges, "strive to be agents of change, driving our organization forward on the path to excellence."

With the resonance of the final words from the visiting lecturer still hanging in the air, the CEO steps forward, his presence commanding attention as he prepares to bring the meeting to a close.

"Ladies and gentlemen," he begins, his voice infused with gratitude and warmth, "I want to extend my sincerest thanks to each and every one of you for your active participation and engagement throughout today's session."

A ripple of appreciation sweeps through the room, a testament to the CEO's acknowledgment of the collective effort invested by all.

"I also want to express my heartfelt gratitude to our esteemed visiting lecturer," the CEO continues, his gaze turning towards the lecturer with genuine appreciation. "Your insights and expertise have truly enriched our discussion, and we are grateful for the invaluable knowledge you have shared with us today."

A murmur of agreement fills the room, echoing the sentiment of gratitude towards the visiting lecturer.

"As we bring this meeting to a close," the CEO says, his voice carrying a note of finality, "let us carry forward the spirit of collaboration, innovation, and continuous improvement that has defined our discussions today."

With a nod of finality, the CEO signals the end of the meeting, prompting the participants to rise from their seats and exchange farewells. As they disperse, the lingering sense of friendship and shared purpose serves as a reminder of the transformative potential that lies ahead, fueled by the collective commitment to excellence and growth.

10

Chapter Ten: Measuring and Evaluating Strengths-Based Initiatives

The Monday morning sun filters through the windows, casting a warm glow over the conference room as the clock strikes 9:00 AM. All eyes turn towards the CEO, who stands at the front of the room, ready to commence the day's proceedings.

"Good morning, everyone," the CEO begins, his voice imbued with energy and purpose. "Today, we have the privilege of delving into a topic of great significance to our organization."

With a swift gesture, the CEO introduces Sibongile, a figure of knowledge and expertise, to lead the discussion on "Key Performance Indicators for Strengths-Based Organizations."

Sibongile wastes no time, stepping forward with confidence and authority. "Thank you, CEO, for the introduction," she says, her voice clear and resolute. "Today, we embark on a journey to explore the intricacies of measuring success in strengths-based organizations."

In the introductory segment, Sibongile lays the groundwork, defining key performance indicators (KPIs) as vital tools for gauging organizational performance. "KPIs," she explains, "serve as guideposts, illuminating the path towards achieving our goals and objectives."

Transitioning seamlessly, she delves into the essence of strengths-based organizations, emphasizing their focus on leveraging individual and collective strengths to drive success. "In a strengths-based organization," she asserts, "every individual's unique talents and capabilities are celebrated and harnessed for the greater good."

With precision, Sibongile navigates through each section of the lecture, dissecting the intricacies of identifying relevant KPIs for strengths-based organizations.

"In assessing organizational goals and objectives," she explains, "we must identify key areas where strengths can contribute to success, and determine specific metrics to measure their impact."

As she delves into KPIs for individual strengths development and team collaboration, Sibongile emphasizes the importance of setting goals, monitoring progress, and fostering effective communication among team members.

"In assessing organizational culture and engagement," she continues, "we must measure employee satisfaction, the impact of strengths-based practices, and the alignment between organizational values and initiatives."

With each passing moment, Sibongile's expertise shines through, guiding the audience through the complexities of measuring success in a strengths-based context.

As she nears the conclusion of her lecture, Sibongile reflects on the importance of implementation, monitoring, evaluation, and continuous improvement in the development and utilization of KPIs.

As Sibongile opens the floor for questions on key performance indicators (KPIs) for strengths-based organizations, the three directors, excluding Smith, eagerly prepare to engage with the topic, their minds brimming with curiosity and a thirst for actionable insights.

Director Johnson, known for her strategic acumen, raises her hand first, her eyes alight with anticipation. "Sibongile, how do we ensure that the KPIs we set align with the unique strengths and objectives of our organization, rather than adopting a one-size-fits-all approach?" she inquires, her tone reflecting a keen awareness of the importance of strategic alignment.

Sibongile nods appreciatively, acknowledging the significance of aligning KPIs with organizational strengths and goals. "Setting KPIs requires a deep understanding of the organization's strengths, objectives, and key areas for improvement. It involves conducting thorough assessments and engaging stakeholders to ensure alignment with strategic priorities," she responds, her words resonating with wisdom and insight.

Director Garcia, renowned for her analytical prowess, raises a question about measuring the effectiveness of strengths-based initiatives. "Sibongile, how can we effectively track and measure the impact of strengths-based approaches on organizational performance and employee engagement?" she asks, her tone reflecting a desire for data-driven insights.

Sibongile listens intently, recognizing the importance of metrics in assessing the success of strengths-based initiatives. "Measuring the effectiveness of strengths-based approaches involves establishing clear metrics, collecting relevant data, and analyzing outcomes to identify areas of improvement and success," she explains, her words underscored by a commitment to accountability and results.

Director Patel, valued for his innovative thinking, poses a question about leveraging technology to enhance KPI tracking. "Sibongile, how can we leverage technology and data analytics to streamline KPI tracking and gain real-time insights into our organization's strengths and performance?" he queries, his tone reflecting a desire for innovative solutions.

Sibongile considers Director Patel's question thoughtfully, recognizing the transformative potential of technology in enhancing KPI tracking. "Leveraging technology involves adopting data-driven platforms and tools that enable real-time monitoring, analysis, and visualization of key metrics. It empowers organizations to make informed decisions and drive continuous improvement," she explains, her words infused with a sense of forward-thinking and adaptability.

With the directors' questions addressed comprehensively, Sibongile prepares to offer her concluding remarks on key performance indicators for strengths-based organizations, confident in the team's ability to leverage data-driven insights to drive organizational success.

"In conclusion," Sibongile says, her voice filled with conviction, "let us embrace the transformative power of data-driven decision-making and commit to leveraging KPIs for the success of our organization."

With a final nod of gratitude to the CEO and the attentive audience, Sibongile concludes her lecture, leaving the room abuzz with inspiration and determination to embark on the journey towards organizational excellence.

As the clock strikes noon, signaling the arrival of the lunch hour, a collective murmur of anticipation fills the room. All eyes turn towards the CEO, who stands at the front, ready to make the much-awaited announcement.

"Ladies and gentlemen," the CEO declares, his voice carrying across the room with authority, "it's time for lunch."

A wave of relief and excitement washes over the attendees, their anticipation for the upcoming break deep. With a nod from the CEO, the room erupts into movement as participants begin to gather their belongings, exchanging smiles and pleasantries as they prepare to depart for lunch.

Amidst the hustle and bustle, the CEO's announcement serves as a welcome reprieve, offering a moment of respite and relaxation amidst the day's proceedings. With anticipation for the delicious meal ahead, the attendees eagerly make their way towards the exit, ready to recharge and refuel before returning for the afternoon session.

As the clock strikes 1:00 PM, the room gradually falls silent, anticipation hanging in the air like a thick fog. All eyes turn towards Sibongile, who stands poised and ready to continue her lecture on "Assessing the Impact of Strengths-Based Interventions."

"Thank you for reconvening," Sibongile begins, her voice steady and purposeful. "Let us delve deeper into the critical process of evaluating the impact of strengths-based interventions."

With precision, she launches into the introductory segment, meticulously laying the groundwork for the discussion ahead. "Strengths-based interventions," she explains, "are strategic initiatives designed to leverage individuals' strengths for personal and organizational development."

The importance of assessing their impact, she emphasizes, cannot be overstated. "It is through assessment," she declares, "that we gain insights into the effectiveness of our interventions and drive continuous improvement."

Transitioning seamlessly, Sibongile delves into the crucial step of establishing clear objectives for strengths-based interventions. "By defining specific goals and clarifying desired outcomes," she asserts, "we set the stage for meaningful assessment and evaluation."

With conviction, she moves on to the identification of key metrics, stressing the importance of selecting both quantitative and qualitative measures to capture the full spectrum of impact.

"In our quest to assess impact," she explains, "we must employ a variety of data collection methods, including surveys, interviews, and the analysis of performance metrics and organizational data."

As she guides the audience through the process of analyzing results, Sibongile's expertise shines through. "It is through interpretation and analysis," she states, "that we uncover trends, patterns, and correlations that inform our understanding of intervention effectiveness."

Stakeholder feedback, she emphasizes, is invaluable in this process, providing nuanced insights that enrich the assessment process and drive continuous improvement.

With each passing moment, Sibongile's passion for the topic becomes increasingly evident. "Through reporting and communication," she asserts, "we disseminate assessment findings and translate them into actionable insights for decision-making and future actions."

As she nears the conclusion of her lecture, Sibongile leaves the audience with a resounding call to action. "Let us commit," she urges, "to ongoing assessment and enhancement of our strengths-based approaches, driven by data-driven decision-making and a relentless pursuit of excellence."

As Sibongile concludes her presentation on assessing the

impact of strengths-based interventions, she opens the floor for questions from the three directors, excluding Smith. Each director, eager to delve deeper into the topic, raises insightful inquiries, poised to uncover actionable insights.

Director Johnson, known for his strategic thinking, raises his hand first, her gaze focused and determined. "Sibongile, how do we differentiate between correlation and causation when assessing the impact of strengths-based interventions on organizational outcomes?" he asks, his voice resonating with a desire for clarity and precision.

Sibongile nods thoughtfully, acknowledging the importance of distinguishing between correlation and causation in impact assessment. "Differentiating between correlation and causation requires robust data analysis and careful consideration of confounding variables. It involves conducting rigorous research and employing statistical methods to draw valid conclusions," she explains, her response reflecting a commitment to rigorous methodology and evidence-based practice.

Director Garcia, renowned for her analytical skills, poses a question about measuring intangible outcomes. "Sibongile, how do we quantify the impact of strengths-based interventions on factors such as employee morale and organizational culture, which are often difficult to measure?" she inquires, her tone reflective of a desire for practical measurement techniques.

Sibongile listens attentively, recognizing the challenges associated with quantifying intangible outcomes. "Measuring intangible outcomes requires a multi-dimensional approach, incorporating qualitative data, employee feedback, and cultural assessments. It involves using a combination of surveys, interviews, and observational methods to capture the nuances of organizational dynamics," she responds, her words infused with a commitment to holistic evaluation.

Director Patel, known for his innovative thinking, raises a question about leveraging technology for impact assessment. "Sibongile, how can we harness technology and data analytics to enhance our ability to assess the impact of strengths-based interventions in real time?" he queries, his tone reflecting a desire for cutting-edge solutions.

Sibongile considers Director Patel's question thoughtfully, recognizing the transformative potential of technology in impact assessment. "Leveraging technology involves adopting data-driven platforms and tools that enable real-time monitoring, analysis, and visualization of key metrics. It empowers organizations to gain timely insights and make informed decisions," she explains, her response underscored by a commitment to innovation and continuous improvement.

With the directors' questions addressed comprehensively, Sibongile prepares to offer her concluding remarks on assessing the impact of strengths-based interventions, confident in the team's ability to leverage data-driven insights to drive organizational success.

With a final nod of gratitude to the attentive audience, Sibongile concludes her lecture, leaving the room abuzz with inspiration and determination to embark on the journey towards enhanced effectiveness and impact in strengths-based interventions.

As the tea break draws to a close, the anticipation in the room heightens, signaling the resumption of Sibongile's lecture on "Iterative Improvement in Strengths-Based Practices." With a renewed sense of focus and determination, the attendees settle back into their seats, eager to glean insights from the continuation of the session.

Sibongile steps forward once more, her presence commanding attention as she prepares to delve deeper into the topic at hand. "Thank you all for returning," she begins, her voice carrying a note of enthusiasm. "Let us now explore the transformative power of iterative improvement in strengths-based practices."

In the introductory segment, Sibongile elucidates the concept of iterative improvement, painting a vivid picture of its significance in fostering continuous growth and development. "Iterative improvement," she explains, "is the process of making small, incremental changes over time to enhance effectiveness and efficiency."

The importance of applying this approach to strengths-based practices, she emphasizes, cannot be overstated. "In a dynamic and ever-evolving landscape," she asserts, "iterative improvement enables us to adapt and thrive, leveraging our strengths to their fullest potential."

With clarity and conviction, Sibongile guides the audience through the various facets of iterative improvement, starting with the crucial step of continuous assessment. "By regularly evaluating our strengths-based practices," she states, "we can pinpoint areas for improvement and chart a course towards excellence."

Next, she explores the importance of feedback mechanisms in the iterative improvement process, stressing the value of soliciting input from stakeholders and incorporating their insights into practice refinement.

"Data-driven decision-making," she continues, "serves as a cornerstone of iterative improvement, enabling us to analyze data to inform improvements and track progress over time."

As she delves into the principles of flexibility and adaptability, Sibongile underscores the importance of adjusting strategies based on feedback and embracing change as opportunities for growth.

"Collaboration and communication," she emphasizes, "are essential for fostering a culture of iterative improvement, encouraging teamwork and ensuring that changes are effectively communicated and implemented."

In the subsequent segments, Sibongile explores the role of training and development in enhancing skills and supporting employees in leveraging strengths effectively. She also highlights the significance of celebrating successes and nurturing a culture of continuous improvement.

As she nears the conclusion of her lecture, Sibongile leaves the audience with a resounding call to action. "Let us commit," she urges, "to embracing adaptability, fostering collaboration, and celebrating our collective achievements as we embark on the journey of iterative improvement for organizational success."

With a final nod of gratitude to the engaged audience, Sibongile concludes her lecture, leaving the room abuzz with inspiration and determination to embrace the principles of iterative improvement in their strengths-based practices.

As the discussions wind down and the meeting draws to a close, all eyes turn towards the CEO, who stands at the front of the room, ready to deliver the final remarks. The CEO's presence commands attention, and a hush falls over the assembled participants, eager to hear his words.

"Ladies and gentlemen," the CEO begins, his voice resonating with warmth and gratitude, "I want to extend my sincerest thanks to each and every one of you for your active participation and valuable contributions throughout today's meeting."

A ripple of appreciation spreads through the room, echoing the CEO's sentiments as nods of agreement and murmurs of thanks reverberate among the attendees.

"I also want to express my heartfelt gratitude to our esteemed visiting lecturer," the CEO continues, turning towards the front row where the lecturer sits, "for sharing your expertise and insights with us. Your contribution has enriched our discussions and provided valuable guidance as we navigate the complexities of our work."

A round of applause erupts from the audience, a tangible expression of appreciation for the lecturer's invaluable input and expertise.

"As we bring this meeting to a close," the CEO says, his voice carrying a note of finality, "let us carry forward the spirit of collaboration, innovation, and continuous improvement that has defined our discussions today."

With a nod of finality, the CEO signals the end of the meeting, prompting the participants to rise from their seats and exchange farewells. As they disperse, the lingering sense of friendship and shared purpose serves as a reminder of the transformative potential that lies ahead, fueled by the collective commitment to excellence and growth.

11

Chapter Eleven: Case Studies: Examples of Strengths-Based Organizations

As the sun rises on a crisp Tuesday morning, casting golden hues through the windows of the conference room, anticipation fills the air. At exactly 9:00 AM, the CEO strides into the room, radiating an aura of authority and enthusiasm. With a welcoming smile, he greets each participant, setting the stage for an enlightening discussion on "Real-Life Examples of Organizations Embracing Strengths."

"Ladies and gentlemen, good morning," the CEO begins, his voice commanding attention. "Today, we embark on a journey to explore the transformative power of strengths-based approaches in organizations."

In the introductory segment, the CEO provides a succinct overview of the strengths-based approach, highlighting its emphasis on leveraging individual talents and abilities for collective success. "At the heart of strengths-based practices," he explains, "lies a profound understanding of the unique strengths and capabilities of each individual."

Turning to the importance of real-life examples, he emphasizes their significance in illustrating the practical application and benefits of strengths-based approaches. "By examining how leading organizations embrace strengths," he declares, "we gain valuable insights into effective implementation strategies and their impact on organizational success."

With a seamless transition, the CEO delves into the first real-life example: Google. "Google, renowned for its innovative culture, exemplifies the power of strengths-based practices through initiatives such as 'Project Oxygen,'" he elaborates. "By focusing on individual development and team effectiveness, and utilizing data-driven insights to enhance employee engagement, Google has cultivated a workplace where strengths flourish and innovation thrives."

Continuing his exploration, the CEO shifts the spotlight to Deloitte, highlighting the firm's implementation of the "Deloitte Leadership Academy." "Deloitte's emphasis on leadership development and talent management, coupled with the integration of strengths-based coaching and feedback, underscores the organization's commitment to nurturing and leveraging the strengths of its workforce," he explains.

With each example, the CEO paints a vivid picture of organizations embracing strengths. From Zappos' cultivation of a strengths-based culture through "Zappos Insights" to Gallup's development and dissemination of the "StrengthsFinder" assessment, and Microsoft's adoption of a strengths-based approach in its "Growth Mindset" initiative, the audience is captivated by the breadth and depth of application.

As the CEO concludes his lecture, he offers a heartfelt recap of the real-life examples discussed, highlighting the insights gained from their implementation strategies. "May these examples inspire us to embrace strengths-based practices in our own organizations," he concludes, his words resonating with hope and determination. "For it is through leveraging the unique talents and abilities of each individual that we can truly unlock the full potential of our teams and organizations."

As the clock strikes 1:00 PM, the team reconvenes, their minds refreshed and their spirits invigorated after a satisfying lunch break. Anticipation fills the room as they gather for the final lecture of the day, awaiting the wisdom that the CEO is about to impart.

With a commanding presence, the CEO takes the floor, his demeanor exuding authority and wisdom. "Good afternoon, everyone," he begins, his voice carrying a tone of earnestness. "As we embark on the last leg of our journey today, I want to delve into a topic that lies at the heart of organizational growth and development: Lessons Learned and Best Practices."

In the introductory segment, the CEO sets the stage by highlighting the importance of reflecting on past experiences. "In our fast-paced world, it's easy to overlook the value of pausing to reflect on our journey," he explains. "However, it is through this reflection that we uncover valuable insights that can shape our future endeavors."

With a seamless transition, the CEO delves into the first section: Lessons Learned. "Identifying key insights from past experiences is essential for our growth," he asserts. "By analyzing both our successes and failures, we uncover valuable takeaways that guide us towards success."

He stresses the importance of documenting these lessons learned, emphasizing that they serve as a compass for future endeavors, guiding the organization towards success.

Moving on to Best Practices, the CEO defines the term within the organizational context. "Best practices are not just strategies; they are tried-and-tested methodologies that yield optimal results," he elucidates. "Identifying and documenting these practices within our organization ensures consistency and efficiency in our operations."

With fervor, the CEO presents case studies, real-life examples that illustrate the application of lessons learned and best practices in action. "These case studies provide invaluable insights that inform our decision-making and shape our approach to organizational development," he remarks.

As the CEO navigates through the topics of Continuous Improvement, Leadership, and Communication, he underscores the pivotal role of these principles in fostering a culture of growth and excellence within the organization. "Continuous improvement isn't just a goal; it's a mindset," he declares. "By incorporating lessons learned and best practices into our daily operations, we pave the way for sustained success."

In the concluding segment, the CEO offers a heartfelt recap of the key concepts discussed, emphasizing the value of reflection and continuous improvement. "Let us commit to prioritizing learning and adaptation," he implores, his voice resonating with conviction. "For it is through our collective efforts that we pave the way for long-term success and prosperity."

With a resounding call to action, the CEO concludes the lecture, leaving the team inspired and empowered to embark on their journey of growth and excellence.

As the CEO draws the meeting to a close, a sense of gratitude permeates the room, enveloping each participant in warmth and appreciation. With a gentle yet commanding presence, the CEO stands before the gathered team, his gaze sweeping across the faces of those assembled.

"Before we part ways," the CEO begins, his voice carrying a tone of sincerity and appreciation, "I want to take a moment to express my heartfelt thanks to each and every one of you."

A wave of quiet anticipation washes over the room as the CEO pauses, allowing his words to sink in, acknowledging the collective effort and dedication that has characterized the meeting.

"Your presence here today has been invaluable," he continues, his words resonating with genuine appreciation. "Your insights, contributions, and unwavering commitment have truly made a difference."

A ripple of nods and smiles spreads through the room, a silent acknowledgment of the CEO's words and a testament to the collaborative spirit that permeates the organization.

"As we bring this meeting to a close," the CEO concludes, his voice imbued with a sense of finality, "let us carry forward the momentum and enthusiasm generated here today. Together, we will continue to strive for excellence and achieve great things."

With a final nod of gratitude, the CEO bids farewell to the gathered team, his words echoing in their minds as they disperse, each carrying with them a renewed sense of purpose and determination.

12

Chapter Twelve: Charting the Future of Strengths-Based Organizations

As the soft morning light filters through the windows, casting a gentle glow upon the room, the team gathers in anticipation of the day's proceedings. With the clock striking 9:00 AM, the CEO strides into the room, his presence commanding attention and respect.

"Good morning, everyone," the CEO begins, his voice resonating with warmth and sincerity. "Today, as we gather, let us take a moment to embark on a journey of introspection and reflection."

In the introductory segment, the CEO sets the stage for deep introspection, highlighting the importance of pausing to reflect on the journey traveled thus far. "In the hustle and bustle of our daily lives, it's easy to lose sight of the path we've walked," he muses. "Yet, it is in moments of reflection that we gain clarity and perspective, guiding us forward on our journey."

With a nod of encouragement, the CEO delves into the heart of the discussion: Acknowledgment of Achievements. "Let us take a moment to celebrate our collective successes and accomplishments," he declares, his voice filled with pride. "From the smallest victories to the most significant milestones, each achievement has played a vital role in shaping our journey."

With reverence, the CEO transitions to the Lessons Learned segment, urging the team to glean insights from both triumphs and tribulations. "Through careful analysis of our successes and failures, we uncover valuable lessons that illuminate our path forward," he explains. "It is in embracing these lessons that we grow stronger and wiser."

Next, the CEO bravely confronts the Challenges Faced, acknowledging the obstacles encountered along the way. "We have weathered storms and navigated rough seas," he reflects, his voice tinged with determination. "Yet, through resilience and perseverance, we have emerged stronger than ever."

With a sense of pride, the CEO delves into the Growth and Development segment, highlighting the personal and professional evolution experienced by each team member. "Our journey has been one of continuous growth and learning," he remarks, his words echoing with conviction. "Each step forward has paved the way for newfound skills, knowledge, and a transformed mindset."

In a poignant moment, the CEO expresses Gratitude and Appreciation towards the support networks and collaborators who have stood by the team's side. "To our mentors, colleagues, and supporters, we owe a debt of gratitude," he declares, his voice filled with heartfelt appreciation. "Their unwavering support has been the cornerstone of our success."

Looking ahead with unwavering optimism, the CEO paints a vivid picture of the future based on reflections, outlining goals and aspirations for continued growth and success. "As we gaze towards the horizon, let us do so with hope and determination," he urges, his words igniting a spark of inspiration within each team member.

In the concluding segment, the CEO offers a heartfelt recap of the key reflections shared, emphasizing the value of introspection and growth. "Let us carry forward the lessons learned and the wisdom gained," he concludes, his voice resonating with conviction. "For it is through continued learning and development that we pave the way for a brighter, more prosperous future."

As the clock strikes 1:00 PM, the team reconvenes, their minds buzzing with anticipation for the final session of the day. Energized from the brief respite of lunch, they gather once more, ready to delve into the future of leadership with the CEO at the helm.

With a commanding presence, the CEO takes the floor, his demeanor radiating a sense of purpose and vision. "Good afternoon, everyone," he begins, his voice resonating with authority. "As we embark on our final discussion today, let us peer into the horizon and explore the trends and innovations shaping the landscape of strengths-based leadership."

In the introductory segment, the CEO sets the stage for an exploration of future trends, emphasizing the importance of foresight and adaptability. "In today's dynamic world, staying ahead in strengths-based leadership is paramount," he asserts. "Let us prepare ourselves to embrace the challenges and opportunities that lie ahead."

With seamless eloquence, the CEO navigates through the emerging trends in strengths-based leadership, painting a picture of the evolving landscape. "We are witnessing a shift towards remote and flexible work arrangements," he explains. "Coupled with an increased emphasis on diversity, equity, and inclusion, these trends are reshaping the way we lead and manage."

Transitioning seamlessly, the CEO delves into the realm of innovations, highlighting the transformative potential of personalized coaching, gamification, and AI-driven talent management. "These innovations hold the key to unlocking the full potential of our workforce," he proclaims, his words igniting a spark of curiosity among the listeners.

As the discussion progresses, the CEO shines a spotlight on the profound impact of these trends and innovations on organizational culture. "By promoting a strengths-based culture and cultivating psychological safety, we foster an environment where innovation and collaboration thrive," he declares, his conviction palpable.

Yet, amidst the promise of the future, the CEO acknowledges the challenges that lie ahead, from addressing resistance to change to harnessing the potential of emerging technologies. "These challenges are not insurmountable," he reassures, his voice unwavering. "With the right strategies and a steadfast commitment to growth, we can turn these challenges into opportunities for success."

In the concluding segment, the CEO offers a heartfelt recap of the future trends and innovations in strengths-based leadership. "Let us embrace adaptability and forward-thinking," he implores, his words echoing with a sense of urgency. "For it is through our collective efforts that we will chart a course towards organizational success."

With a resounding call to action, the CEO concludes the discussion, leaving the team inspired and empowered to embrace the future of leadership with confidence and determination.

As the final echoes of the CEO's words fade into the room,

a profound sense of gratitude fills the air, intertwining with the lingering anticipation of what lies ahead. With a gentle yet commanding presence, the CEO stands before the assembled participants, his gaze warm and appreciative.

"Before we part ways," he begins, his voice carrying a tone of sincerity and appreciation, "I want to extend my heartfelt thanks to each and every one of you."

A wave of quiet acknowledgment washes over the room as the CEO pauses, allowing his words to sink in, recognizing the dedication and commitment displayed by each individual throughout the extensive period of lectures spanning almost two weeks.

"Your unwavering commitment and active participation have been truly commendable," the CEO continues, his words infused with genuine gratitude. "It is your enthusiasm and engagement that have made these lectures a resounding success."

As he speaks, nods of agreement and smiles of appreciation ripple through the audience, a silent testament to the CEO's words and the collective effort invested in the journey of learning and growth.

"Your contributions have not gone unnoticed," the CEO affirms, his voice unwavering with conviction. "Your commitment to personal and professional development is a testament to your dedication to excellence."

With a final nod of gratitude, the CEO bids farewell to the participants, his words echoing in their minds as they disperse, each carrying with them a renewed sense of purpose and determination.

In the world of Howard, the CEO, leisure is not just a luxury; it's a meticulously planned escape from the rigors of corporate life. With the precision of a master strategist,

Howard orchestrates his leisure time to perfection, ensuring every moment is filled with joy, relaxation, and the company of those he holds dear.

The following Saturday as the sun begins its slow descent towards the horizon, casting a warm glow over the landscape, Howard gathers his trusted directors for a round of golf at the prestigious country club. Dressed in tailored golfing attire, they stride purposefully onto the manicured greens, their spirits buoyant with anticipation.

With each swing of the club, Howard and his companions immerse themselves in the timeless rhythm of the game, their laughter mingling with the gentle rustle of the breeze. Amidst the lush surroundings, amidst the friendship of his fellow players, Howard finds a sense of peace and renewal.

But as the afternoon sun gives way to the soft hues of twilight, Howard and his directors decide to take their leisurely pursuits to the next level. With a quick change of attire, they make their way to a cozy sports bar, the air alive with the energy of excited fans and the tantalizing aroma of pub fare.

Settling into plush leather chairs, they raise their glasses in a toast to friendship and relaxation, their eyes fixed on the large screen broadcasting a thrilling soccer match. As the tension mounts and the crowd erupts into cheers, Howard and his companions become swept up in the excitement, their shouts of encouragement echoing through the room.

Amidst the pulse-pounding action of the game, Howard and his directors find a rare moment of respite, a chance to unwind and bond outside the confines of the boardroom. In this shared experience, amidst the laughter and friendship, they forge memories that will last a lifetime, reminding themselves that even in the fast-paced world of business, there is always time for leisure and friendship.

About the Author

Goodson Mumba is a multifaceted individual known for his diverse expertise and prolific contributions across various fields. As an infopreneur, Management Consultant, thought leader, and spiritual leader, he has inspired countless individuals through his insightful teachings and impactful writings. Mumba is also an accomplished author, with several notable works to his name, including "Understanding Corporate Worship," "The Years I Spent in a Week," "Management By Harmony," "The CEO's Diary," "Change to Change" and "Creative Thinking for results" His literary works span topics ranging from business management to personal development and spirituality, reflecting his broad range of interests and insights.

With a Master of Business Leadership (MBL) and a Bachelor of Arts in Theology (BTh), Mumba brings a unique blend of business acumen and spiritual wisdom to his work. His educational background is further enriched by a Group Diploma in Management Studies, providing him with a solid foundation in organizational dynamics and leadership principles. Additionally, Mumba holds diplomas in Education Psychology, Leadership and Management Styles, Organizational Behaviour, Financial Accounting, Economic Growth and Development, and Project Management, showcasing his commitment to continuous learning and professional development.

Mumba's expertise extends beyond traditional academic disciplines, encompassing areas such as Neuro-Linguistic Programming (NLP) and Positive Psychology. His diverse skill set is complemented by a range of certifications, including Creative Problem Solving and Decision Making, Life Coaching Fundamentals and Techniques, Professional Life Coaching, and Performance Management System Design. These certifications reflect Mumba's dedication to equipping himself with the tools and knowledge necessary to empower others and drive positive change.

As an author, Mumba's writings reflect his deep understanding of human nature, organizational dynamics, and spiritual principles. His works offer practical insights, actionable strategies, and inspirational guidance for individuals seeking personal growth, professional success, and spiritual fulfillment. Mumba's holistic approach to life and leadership resonates with readers worldwide, making him a respected figure in both the business and spiritual communities.

Overall, Goodson Mumba's diverse background, extensive knowledge, and profound insights make him a sought-after speaker, mentor, and author. His commitment to excellence, lifelong learning, and service to others continues to inspire individuals to unlock their full potential and lead lives of purpose and significance.

Goodson Mumba is renowned for initiating the concept of

Management by Harmony, revolutionizing traditional management practices with a focus on balanced and holistic approaches. He has authored two influential books on this subject: "Introduction to Management by Harmony" and its sequel, "Management by Harmony."

Mumba's work has significantly impacted the field, offering innovative strategies for fostering organizational harmony and efficiency. His contributions continue to shape contemporary management theories and practices.

www.ingramcontent.com/pod-product-compliance
Lightning Source LLC
Chambersburg PA
CBHW071829210526
45479CB00001B/62